ILLUSTRATORS 31

From the exhibition held in the galleries of the
Society of Illustrators Museum of American Illustration
128 East 63rd Street, New York, NY 10021
February 1 – April 12, 1989

Society of Illustrators, Inc.
128 East 63rd Street
New York, NY 10021

ISBN 0-8230-5842-5
Library of Congress Catalog Card No. 59-10849

Distributors to the trade in the United States and
Canada:
Watson-Guptill Publications
1515 Broadway, New York, NY 10036

Distributed throughout the rest of the world by:
Hearst Books International
105 Madison Avenue, New York, NY 10016

Publisher:
Madison Square Press
10 East 23rd Street, New York, NY 10010

Editor: Arpi Ermoyan
Designer: Paul Gamarello
Typography: Arnold & Debel

Printed in Japan

Photo Credits: *Guy Billout* by Karl Memecek, *Blair
Drawson* by Kevin Westenberg, *Erté* by Robert Skinner,
Arnie Levin by Susan Ely, *Alma Phipps* by Henry Wolf

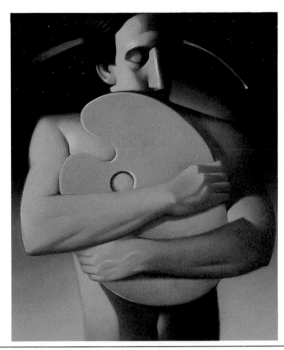

THE SOCIETY OF ILLUSTRATORS
ILLUSTRATORS 31
THIRTY FIRST ANNUAL OF AMERICAN ILLUSTRATION

PUBLISHED FOR THE

SOCIETY OF ILLUSTRATORS

BY

MADISON SQUARE PRESS
NEW YORK

PRESIDENT'S MESSAGE

This 31st Society of Illustrators Annual is a record of the only national juried exhibition of illustration representing all the various facets of this unique art form. That is why this annual is different from all the others.

The Annual has been produced by many people—members of the Society and non-members—who gave their time and talents because of their dedication to the art of illustration. They deserve recognition and our appreciation for the beautiful design and the high quality of this book. Their contribution is most welcome.

An innovation this year is the addition of the artists' telephone numbers, adding to the usefulness of this volume.

And, of course, the artists represented here who have contributed to the Society at large in so many ways through their work, are to be congratulated. Out of 8,000 entries a little over 500 pieces of art were chosen for the exhibition.

These annuals not only record the history of American illustration, they are a constant source of inspiration.

I never tire of looking through them.

Diane Dillon
President, 1987-1989

Portrait by Paul Davis

THE SOCIETY OF ILLUSTRATORS HALL OF FAME

Each year the Society of Illustrators elects to its Hall of Fame those artists who have made an outstanding contribution to the art of illustration throughout the years.

The list of previous winners is truly a ''Who's Who'' of illustration. Former presidents of the Society meet annually to elect those who will be so honored.

Short biographies of the recipients of this award, along with examples of their work, are presented in the following pages.

HALL OF FAME 1989

Erté
John Held Jr.*
Arthur Ignatius Keller*

HALL OF FAME 1958-1988

Norman Rockwell 1958
Dean Cornwell 1959
Harold Von Schmidt 1959
Fred Cooper 1960
Floyd Davis 1961
Edward Wilson 1962
Walter Biggs 1963
Arthur William Brown 1964
Al Parker 1965
Al Dorne 1966
Robert Fawcett 1967
Peter Helck 1968
Austin Briggs 1969
Rube Goldberg 1970
Stevan Dohanos 1971
Ray Prohaska 1972
Jon Whitcomb 1973
Tom Lovell 1974
Charles Dana Gibson* 1974
N.C. Wyeth* 1974
Bernie Fuchs 1975
Maxfield Parrish* 1975
Howard Pyle* 1975
John Falter 1976
Winslow Homer* 1976
Harvey Dunn* 1976
Robert Peak 1977
Wallace Morgan* 1977
J.C. Leyendecker* 1977
Coby Whitmore 1978

Norman Price* 1978
Frederic Remington* 1978
Ben Stahl 1979
Edwin Austin Abbey* 1979
Lorraine Fox* 1979
Saul Tepper 1980
Howard Chandler Christy* 1980
James Montgomery Flagg* 1980
Stan Galli 1981
Frederic R. Gruger* 1981
John Gannam* 1981
John Clymer 1982
Henry P. Raleigh* 1982
Eric (Carl Erickson)* 1982
Mark English 1983
Noel Sickles* 1983
Franklin Booth* 1983
Neysa Moran McMein* 1984
John LaGatta* 1984
James Williamson* 1984
Charles Marion Russell* 1985
Arthur Burdett Frost* 1985
Robert Weaver 1985
Rockwell Kent* 1986
Al Hirschfeld 1986
Haddon Sundblom* 1987
Maurice Sendak 1987
René Bouché* 1988
Pruett Carter* 1988
Robert T. McCall 1988

*Presented posthumously

HALL OF FAME COMMITTEE

Willis Pyle/*Chairman*
Past Presidents of the Society:
Harry Carter, D.L. Cramer, Stevan Dohanos,
Charles McVicker, Howard Munce, Alvin J. Pimsler,
Warren Rogers, Shannon Stirnweis, David K. Stone,
John Witt

HALL OF FAME 1989
ERTÉ

To the generations who long ago embraced the styles of Art Nouveau and Art Deco, and to those who came later to discover anew their virtues, the name Erté is legendary. His designs for women's fashions, jewelry, theatrical costumes and stage and screen set decoration have thrilled millions the world over through a career which has spanned seven decades. He is the quintessential prophet of fashion (having employed the unisex look some four decades before its time) and to many his very name is synonymous with style. His intense and meticulously executed illustrative work combines the rhythmical sensuality of a Beardsley with the breathless elegance of a Persian miniature. His colorful visions, rendered in gouache and accented with metallic paints, bristle with fanciful charm and evoke in the viewer a passion for far-off times and exotic places.

Born Romain de Tirtoff in St. Petersburg in 1892, Erté was the privileged son of Russian aristocrats in that affluent era before the Revolution. Through his parents' indulgences, Erté was exposed to the opera and the ballet at an early age, thus cultivating in him an appreciation for music and the theater. He studied under the noted Russian portraitist S.E. Repine and later, after relocating to Paris, enrolled at the Academie Julian where he studied briefly with the French painter Jean-Paul Laurens. His artistic sensibilities, however, were brought into focus while in the employ of Paul Pioret, a leading producer of women's fashions for whom he worked as a dress designer in 1913. The pseudonym Erté evolved from the earlier use of his initials R.T. and first appeared in print during his tenure with Pioret. Shortly after moving to Monte Carlo the following year he became a contributor to the magazine, *Harper's Bazar* (later spelled *Bazaar*), attracted the attention of such Broadway luminaries as Florenz Ziegfield, George White, Earl Carroll, and the Schuberts. He worked for them all, producing an astonishing number of fresh and original designs until the Great Depression descended upon Broadway in the closing months of 1929.

His work in *Harper's Bazar* also brought the patronage of publisher William Randolph Hearst, who eventually employed his talents for the Hearst motion picture company, Cosmopolitan Films. Erté's much heralded arrival in Hollywood in 1925 came at the invitation of Hearst's friend, movie mogul Louis B. Mayer, who committed the artist to an exclusive contract. Many of the projects offered as inducements, however, never materialized and after only 18 months Erté left the United States in frustration. Despite his difficulties during this period, his contributions to MGM's 1926 version of *Ben-Hur,* to Browning's *The Mystic,* and to King Vidor's *La Boheme* have helped to establish these film works as classics of the silent screen.

In the mid-1960s, while researching a book on the Parisian music hall, writer Jacques Damase discovered Erté's art and, to his delight, further learned that the artist had diligently retrieved and hoarded his work over the years, thus preserving a significant historical record which would otherwise have been lost. At Damase's suggestion the Grosvenor Galleries in London and New York hosted exhibitions of Erté's art in 1967, thereby reintroducing it to a world which had recently reawakened to the elegance and style of an earlier time.

The Society of Illustrators is pleased to recognize the extraordinary body of work amassed by this inventive and prolific artist by inducting him into its Hall of Fame. At ninety-seven this remarkable individual continues to produce, thus expanding his already considerable influence upon the culture and style of the Twentieth Century.

Vincent DiFate
Permanent Collection Chairman

Harper's Bazar cover, March 1919

HALL OF FAME 1989

JOHN HELD JR. (1889-1958)

The political and social history of the 1920s is comprehensively recorded in dusty rows of bound volumes on the library shelves, but to discover the *spirit* of that decade one should look at the work of John Held Jr. He depicted a liberated post-World War I generation that rejected the old values and who eagerly embraced jazz, the Charleston, bathtub gin, bobbed hair, necking parties, short skirts and bell-bottom trousers.

No one depicted it all better than Held. Humor was his forte. His brittle, irreverent black and white drawings appeared in all the contemporary magazines, from *College Humor, Judge, Life* and *Cosmopolitan* to *Vanity Fair* and *The New Yorker*. He also produced many cover designs in colorful gouache. Advertisers clamored for his services; his hallmark conferred distinction to such products as Van Heusen collars, Packard automobiles and Tintex home dyes. One frustrated advertiser, turned down because of Held's overloaded schedule, gave him a blank check to fill in his own price.

All this success did not come easily. Held was born a Mormon in 1889 in Salt lake City. As a teenager, he learned to make engravings for his father's stationery business and also learned about the seamy side of saloon life and brothels in a wide-open frontier era.

Many of these subjects were pictured in parody and published later at the instigation of Harold Ross, a childhood chum, in the pages of *The New Yorker*.

To solicit his first work in New York, Held sent his pretty young wife out to call on the art editors. She successfully sold the work as her own, and Held's early work was signed "Myrtle." After the couple split up, Held was able to reveal his own identity. As his work became more popular and the money began to roll in, Held lived the life he depicted. He had residences in New York and Florida, and a farm in Weston, Connecticut. He also entertained lavishly and went through three wives.

The 1929 stock market crash brought a precipitate end to the gaiety. The consequent depression squeezed everyone's economic resources. Bankruptcies and suicides took their toll; there was very little to laugh about. Held's humor was out of keeping with the grim realities of the thirties and publishers stopped buying his work.

Held had lost most of his money to the fraudulent scheme of Ivar Kreugar, the Swedish match king, and the Depression hit him doubly hard. He wrote and illustrated several books (which did not pay well), a play (which was not produced), and turned to sculpture. This was a labor of love which involved animals, such as he had raised on his farm. They were a critical success, but he sold almost no casts. He also had started a forge, making weather vanes, signs, andirons and other handsomely designed implements out of wrought iron. Among his other activities were stints as artist-in-residence at Harvard and the University of Georgia, experiments with pottery, and wartime work at the U.S. Signal Corps drawing radar equipment. He happily spent his remaining years with his fourth wife, running a small but nearly self-sufficient farm in Belmar, New Jersey.

As an artist, Held's style was unique and personal. His pen line was fine and precise, augmented by judicious areas of solid black. His color was brilliant, often employed in a pointillist manner. But it was his satirical humor that made his art. He certainly had no pretense of being a social historian. However, because he was slightly older than the twenties generation, he was able to observe events with a more detached perspective than the "flaming youth" he depicted. They, in turn, accepted Held's exaggerated portrayals as real and reinforced them by emulation. Thus, Held was both a creator and chronicler and helped to make history while recording it.

Walt Reed
Illustration House

"The Girl He Left Behind," August 1927
Courtesy Illustration House, Inc.

HALL OF FAME 1989
ARTHUR IGNATIUS KELLER (1866-1924)

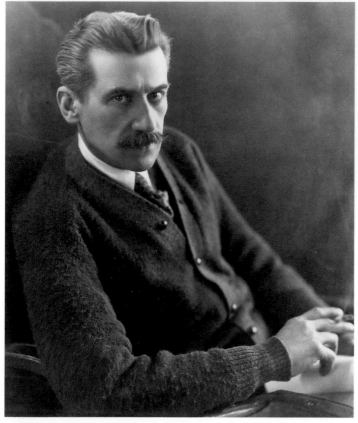

Born in New York of German immigrant parents, Keller at 17 entered the National Academy of Design in New York City to study with Lemuel Wilmarth and Edgar Melville Ward. In order to further his art studies he traveled to Munich in 1890 and spent a year studying under the German classical painter, Ludwig von Loefftz. He became an accomplished artist whose work was compared to the French master Watteau.

Keller decided to use his great talent to pursue a career in illustration. Upon his return to America he was hired by the *New York Herald* as an illustrator. Following this job at the newspaper, he began illustrating for magazines and within two years was working for book publishers as well.

From the turn of the century until his death, his wonderful illustrations graced the pages of the leading periodicals of his time. They included *The Delineator, Cosmopolitan, McClure's, Scribner's, Harper's, Ladies' Home Journal, Century,* and the *Sunday Magazine.*

Keller lived in Riverdale, New York, with his family and summered in Cragsmoor, New York, in the Shawangunk Mountains which was a colony of accomplished artists that included E.L. Henry and C.C. Curran. Keller's homes were filled with antiques, costumes, and a library of reference books. All of these were used to help him create authentic illustrations of the periods they represented. He worked endlessly—sketching, composing, perfecting his art. He made graphic notes about his research, compiling them into a two-volume set of books published in 1920 titled "Figure Studies from Life." He used family members as models and these familiar faces appear in many of his works. As busy as he was, he always found the time to devote to his family whom he dearly loved.

Keller was a charter member of the Society of Illustrators and served as its president in 1903. In 1925 a memorial exhibition was held by the Society of Illustrators in his honor and in January of 1989 a retrospective exhibition.

His numerous awards included the prize for a watercolor in the Philadelphia Art Club in 1899, a Silver Medal in the Paris Exposition in 1900, Bronze Medal for drawing at the Pan American Watercolor Society 1902, Gold and Silver Medals at the St. Louis Exposition in 1904 and the Gold Medal at the Panama Pacific Exposition in 1915. He also won the first Hallgarten composition prize at the National Academy of Design. His painting "At Mass" was purchased by the Munich Academy.

As Walter Jack Duncan said in his glowing tribute to Keller, "Arthur Keller was a true prince. That is to say, he was a 'born artist.' His simplest sketch, every stroke of his brush or pencil, is nervous with artistic energy. One feels it pulsating sturdily through all his multifarious work, through his graceful and sinuous drawings, his exquisite watercolors, his crowded and animated oils." The art critic Royal Cortissoz, upon hearing of Keller's death said, "Whenever the best of American illustrators are recalled, his name will be held in honor among them."

Beverly Sacks

"Marrakesh Street Scene"
Collection of the Society of Illustrators Museum of American Illustration

"The Prince of Graustark"
Collection of the Society of Illustrators Museum of American Illustration

HAMILTON KING AWARD

The Hamilton King Award is presented each year for the finest illustration in the Annual Exhibition done by a member of the Society of Illustrators. The selection is made by former recipients of this award.

HAMILTON KING AWARD 1989
Guy Billout

Where do you get such crazy ideas, Guy Billout? Granted, somewhere in your travels you may have witnessed a bird carrying off a human baby, or a flagpole sprouting tree roots. But where did you dream up a tightrope artist performing on a dotted line, a beachcomber lifting the ocean's edge as easily as a blanket, or shadows defying natural law by impossibly squaring off?

To be fair, it's a conceptual process even the illustrator has trouble pinning down. Billout, who in the last two decades has risen to become the commercial art world's premier purveyor of deadpan, insists his method for deriving visual puns is no more formulaic than groping along a dark tunnel, or rolling a pair of dice.

An ad designer turned commercial illustrator, Billout is clearly no stranger to trying new things; his career path is just as circuitous as his trial-and-error method for deriving new ideas. Born in the remote city of Nevers in southern France to a trade journalist and a bookstore owner, a restless Billout decided, against his parents' wishes, to go into art. "In bour-

geoisie families the idea of making a living in the arts isn't regarded favorably."

He left high school in midstream to study advertising and design at the trade school L'Ecole Des Arts Appliques. It was there he fell in love with a popular French poster artist, Savignac, whose designs "always had some sort of joke," Billout recalls fondly. "I knew I wanted to look like that."

But the aspiring adman's initial attempts to find the right outlet for those early stirrings were unsuccessful. After graduating in 1959, Billout moved to Paris, the undisputed center of French advertising. He managed to quickly break into agency work as a design man and spent his early 20s assisting art directors with layouts and presentations as a *maquettiste* in separate jobs at two large French advertising agencies, Publicis and Thibault Lintas.

However, he found the work less than satisfying. "It took me five years to realize I was not really good as a designer and bored with the work."

It actually took Billout longer than that. Hoping a change of scenery would help him gain more satisfaction in design work, Billout moved to the United States, whose ad campaigns and magazines back then were the envy of the world. Once here, working in the studio of a group of designers he'd befriended, Billout would swap playful little sketches with a fellow designer. The colleague, struck by Billout's visual jokes, convinced him to put design aside and give illustration a whirl.

A newly determined Billout returned temporarily to France. He spent the next three months in seclusion in a Paris apartment, rendering a series that captured the New World impressions of an immigrant. These compositions of photo montage, gouache and marker turned out more like diary than a portfolio. In this early incarnation of the artist's deadpan style, Billout's characters were as aware of New York's nooks and crannies as the artist himself.

Billout returned to America in 1969 clutching his new portfolio of 14 humorous 8-by-8 illustrations. Before long Billout managed to hold court at New York magazine with then art director Milton Glaser, who'd heard through the grapevine about Billout's work. Glaser was impressed by Billout's unusual perspective. "There he was buying my story," Billout glows in reflection. "New York at that time was the toast of the city."

Other magazines soon followed. Advertisers climbed aboard. Billout's career was on its way. "This is the story," Billout reflects, "of a Frenchman realizing some of his dreams by coming to America."

Today, Billout's challenge is to recreate, in a sense, his earlier sojourn. Each day, he must return to the wide-eyed perspective that is his trademark, to face the world with immigrant eyes.

Inspiration flows from a New York City the former Parisian never tires of: sharp afternoon shadows, a potpourri of architecture and skyscraper-tall dreams. To stay fresh, Billout teaches at the School of Visual Arts and Parsons School of Design, where his young charges, in turn, teach him that his vision is not the only one.

David Kalish

HAMILTON KING AWARD 1965-1988

Paul Calle 1965	Leo & Diane Dillon 1977
Bernie Fuchs 1966	Daniel Schwartz 1978
Mark English 1967	William Teason 1979
Robert Peak 1968	Wilson McLean 1980
Alan Cober 1969	Gerald McConnell 1981
Ray Ameijide 1970	Robert Heindel 1982
Miriam Schottland 1971	Robert M. Cunningham 1983
Charles Santore 1972	Braldt Bralds 1984
Dave Blossom 1973	Attila Hejja 1985
Fred Otnes 1974	Doug Johnson 1986
Carol Anthony 1975	Kinuko Y. Craft 1987
Judith Jampel 1976	James McMullan 1988

Reprinted with permission from *Adweek's Winners*

"Directions," *The Atlantic Monthly*

SPECIAL AWARDS 1989

Among those honored by the Society of Illustrators in 1989 were two people who made substantial contributions to the illustration profession. Carol Donner received the Dean Cornwell Achievement Award for her outstanding effort on behalf of artists' rights and fair taxation. Gerald McConnell was presented the Arthur William Brown Recognition Award for his continuing efforts on behalf of the goals and ideals of the Society of Illustrators.

The industry is indebted to the recipients of these awards for helping to raise the profession's and public's awareness and appreciation of the art of illustration.

The Dean Cornwell Achievement Award 1989
Carol Donner

Carol Donner is a respected and successful medical illustrator. Wishing to "give back" to her profession, she became active in the Society of Illustrators, serving on the Membership Committee and as Assistant Treasurer. She then became Legislation Chairman for both the Society and the Association of Medical Illustrators. Little did she foresee that from a quiet, isolated life at the drawing board, she would be catapulted into a national struggle to defeat the tax reform act.

Carol was a key person in mobilizing what she called "The Itty Bitty Artists" and turning them into a "nine hundred pound gorilla who can sleep anywhere he wants to." Her quick wit and sense of humor helped her through the tough spots while her ability to grasp a situation, make decisions, and take action was the key to her success.

She compiled an impressive graphic presentation of artists from various disciplines explaining how complicated and impossible capitalization would be. It won the sympathy of the legislators. She wrote articles, press releases, raised funds, and mobilized artists to send letters and telegrams . . . .and watched her career come to a halt.

One might ask "Why did she do it?" Carol, most likely, asked herself that many times but once involved, she couldn't walk away. She's a fighter.

She has been heard to say, "I'm tired of drawing kidneys," but after sitting at a computer for hours, writing articles, knee-deep in fax messages, the phone ringing every five minutes, those kidneys must have looked pretty good!

One thing for sure, she made many friends and has the satisfaction of knowing that artists around the country benefited from her efforts.

It was no small feat and we want her to know we appreciate it.

Diane Dillon
President, Society of Illustrators

The Arthur William Brown Recognition Award 1989
Gerald McConnell

Why has Jerry McConnell spent so many hours in meetings, some late into the night, some not without tension; so many hours on the roof or in the basement, figuring and fixing; so many months making sure the Annual Books were as good as they possibly could be? The reason, he says, is that he feels illustration has been good to him and this is how he can give something back.

Jerry joined the Society in 1961, just in time to work on the last "Girlie Show." He rose quickly through the Society's ranks, as Gallery Chairman in 1963 to 1966, Annual Show Chairman in '66, and Treasurer the same year.

After a stint as Executive Vice President, he declined nomination to the Presidency and then became House Chairman in 1978, a position he continues to hold today.

Jerry's long association with the Society's publications began in an editorial capacity: he edited *Illustrators 15, 19, 20* and *21*. As coordinator between the Society and Hastings House Publishers he helped usher through Annuals from 1966 through 1980. With *Illustrators 23* he took over as publisher and, two years later produced the first full-color edition. The Annual continues to be published by Madison Square Press.

He coordinated "The Library of American Illustration" volumes, *20 Years of Award Winners* and published Walt and Roger Reed's *100 Years of American Illustration 1880-1980, The New Illustration, Humor* and *Humor 2*.

As an illustrator he participated in 16 national exhibitions, contributed to the Air Force, National Parks and NASA programs and won the Society's Hamilton King Award in 1981.

His service to the community was also expressed when he helped to found the Graphic Artists Guild in 1969 and served on its Board and Executive Committee from then until 1987.

His commitment to the Society is evident in countless ways, from interpreting floor plans to producing beautiful books.

Jill Bossert

CHAIRMAN'S MESSAGE

Working illustrators are constantly aware of the solitude of this profession. The requirement remains to create-on-demand while playing "beat the clock." The challenge remains to make each commission visually exciting. No small task!

As Chairman of the 31st Annual Show I found myself facing tangible proof that we are not working alone— no matter how comforting and romantic that choice can often seem. For October arrived. And the Society's library was suddenly filled to overflow with more than 8,000 entries, the most we've ever received.

Tradition demanded that this iceberg be plumbed and crystalized. For one week celebrated peer jurors explored and selected with dedication: Co-Chairman Abby Merrill and I guided over the ice by the Society's Director, Terry Brown, and his staff.

The result: a unique show and this book recognizing and documenting one year, and rewarding the beauty that comes from dedicated isolation.

Geoffrey Moss
Chairman, *Illustrators 31*

Portrait by Paul Davis

Jurying the Annual Exhibition: How it Works

The most important function of the Annual Exhibition Past Chairmen's Committee is the selection of jurors, which takes place approximately seven months prior to the actual jurying.

A large blackboard is set up with five vertical columns—four for the categories (Advertising, Editorial, Book & Institutional) and one in which to list diverse types of jurors. Every effort is made to create a good mix of talented illustrators and art directors with a wide range of tastes.

The first jurors selected are four Society of Illustrator members, each of whom acts as chairman of one of the categories. Eight additional jurors, including non-Society members, are then selected for each category. In order to avoid bias, jurors are placed in categories other than those from which their primary income is derived professionally. A period of three years must elapse before a juror may serve again. Jurors may not win awards in the category they are judging.

Jurying takes place during four days in October— one category each day. All published entries are set out in stacks of black-and-white, 2-color, full color, and are also broken down according to size within that framework. After the jurors have completed viewing all the entries and have marked those which they feel qualify for the show, the staff sorts them into groups of "like" votes and those with the highest are brought back to be considered for awards.

During the initial voting, jurors are asked to vote silently, without discussion, but when the selection of awards gets underway, jurors are free to express their views on why they think a certain piece merits an award.

The unpublished entries, submitted in slide form, are projected on a screen and voted on by means of a unique voting machine which enables each juror to cast his vote privately. Awards for unpublished pieces are selected the following week by the Balancing Jury.

The Balancing Jury is composed of the current Exhibition Chairman, the four Category Chairmen, and two Past Chairmen. Since each artist accepted in the show is allowed no more than three pieces in a category and no more than five in the entire show (not counting award-winning pieces), it is the Balancing Jury's responsibility to whittle down those exceeding this number.

The Society of Illustrators takes great pride in the integrity with which this show has been managed over the years and intends to maintain this high standard.

Arpi Ermoyan

AWARD WINNERS

BRAD HOLLAND
GOLD MEDAL

TIMOTHY SCOTT JESSELL
GOLD MEDAL

GREG SPALENKA
GOLD MEDAL

CHARLES BRAGG
SILVER MEDAL

DAVID LESH
SILVER MEDAL

SKIP LIEPKE
SILVER MEDAL

STANLEY MELTZOFF
SILVER MEDAL

JURY

WARREN ROGERS, Chairman
Art Director,
Madison Square Press

JOHN BURGOYNE
Illustrator

IVAN CHERMAYEFF
Graphic Designer,
Chermayeff & Geismar

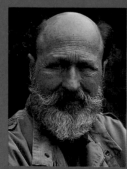

ROBERT M. CUNNINGHAM
Illustrator

ANN MEISEL
Illustrator

ABBY MERRILL
Illustrator

FRED OTNES
Illustrator

BARRIE STERN
Director of Art Department,
Cahners Publishing

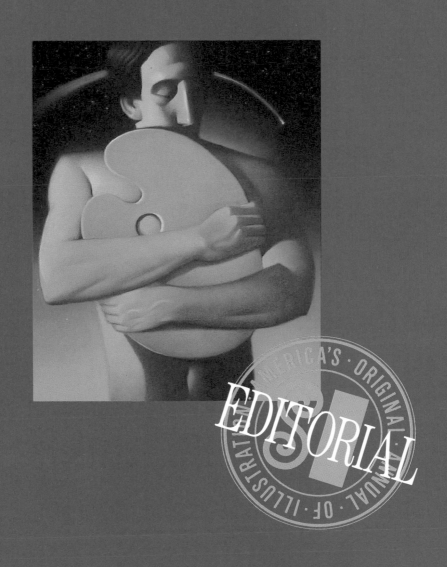

BRAD HOLLAND

A self-taught artist at the age of
13, Holland became a professional
at 17. At 24 he began publishing
in underground newspapers,
which brought him to the attention of *The New York Times* editors. In 1971 he became one of
the founding artists on the
Op-Ed page.

Holland's work has appeared in
major publications throughout
the United States and abroad.
His drawings and paintings have
earned him numerous awards and
have been exhibited in museums
around the world, including the
Louvre in 1974.

1

Art Director: HANS-GEORG
POSPISCHIL

Client: FRANKFURTER ALLGEMEINE
MAGAZIN

TIMOTHY SCOTT JESSELL

A native of Terre Haute, Indiana, Jessell works at The Turner Group, an illustration and design firm in Tulsa, Oklahoma. Using pastels and colored pencils, his realistic illustrations are used in editorial, advertising, and institutional categories.

A 1987 graduate of The University of Tulsa, Jessell is a member of the Art Directors Club of Tulsa, the North American Falconers Association, and the National Wildlife Federation.

Art Director: CLAY TURNER

Client: MARY BRETT & ASSOCIATES

2

ILLUSTRATORS31

GREG SPALENKA

Graduating from the Art Center College of Design in 1982 with a BFA, Spalenka moved from California to New York the following year.

His social-political commentary and illustrations have appeared in most major magazines in the United States.

Greg has received both Gold and Silver Medals from the Society of Illustrators and his work has appeared in the *American Illustration* and *CA* annuals.

Art Director: ANDREW DANISH

Client: THE STANFORD MAGAZINE

3

CHARLES BRAGG

Bragg spent his earliest years traveling in a trailer, having been born to a mother and father who, he claims, were personally responsible for vaudeville's demise.

In the forties he attended Music and Art High School in New York City. But it was some years later, after he was married and had children, that he decided to make a career of his artistic talents.

He now lives and works in Los Angeles, California.

Art Director: **TOM STAEBLER**

Client: **PLAYBOY**

4

DAVID LESH

A native of Indianapolis, Indiana, Lesh attended SMU in Dallas, Texas, after which he returned home, opened a health club and worked for the family business. He began freelancing at night and eventually devoted full time to illustration.

His clients range from *Life, Sports Illustrated* and *The New York Times* to American Express, IBM, E.F. Hutton, and Lotus Development.

Art Director: KAY HARTMANN

Client: CHICAGO BAR ASSOCIATION

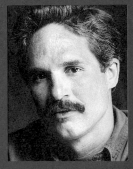

SKIP LIEPKE

Born in Minneapolis, Minnesota, Liepke has lived in the New York area since 1977. Self taught, he feels that living in New York City has allowed him to view firsthand the work of artists he admires— artists such as Velasquez, Whistler, Degas, Chase, Vuillard, Sargent, and others who have influenced his art.

Since moving to New York Liepke has worked for most of the major designers and publications, including covers for *Time*, *Newsweek*, *Forbes*, *Fortune*, and *Sports Illustrated*.

STANLEY MELTZOFF

Born in 1917 in New York City, Meltzoff attended the Institute of Fine Arts at NYU. During WWII he served with the *Stars and Stripes* in Africa and Italy as artist and writer. He resumed illustrating after the war.

Throughout the years Meltzoff has been represented in the Society of Illustrators Annual Shows and won awards.

The Sportsman's Edge gallery in New York City has had exhibitions of the fish paintings for which he is so well known.

Art Director: **VICTOR CLOSI**

Client: **FIELD & STREAM**

7

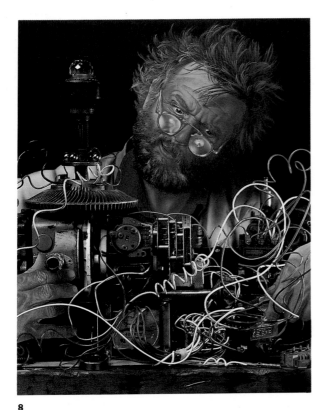

8

9

10

11

8

Artist: **DAVID M. GAADT**

Art Director: ALICE DEGENHARDT

Client: CREATIVE LIVING MAGAZINE

9

Artist: **DOUGLAS ANDELIN**

10

Artist: **DAVID LESH**

Art Director: ROBIN OLDACRE

Client: WORLD LINK MAGAZINE

11

Artist: **JOEL PETER JOHNSON**

Art Director: ANDREW KNER

Client: PRINT

12

Artist: **GREG SPALENKA**

Art Director: MELISSA WASSERMAN

Client: DIMENSIONS

12

13

14

15

16

13

Artist: **MARVIN MATTELSON**

Art Director: RUDY HOGLUND

Client: COMMUNICATION ARTS

14

Artist: **QUANG HO**

Art Director: SANDRA MAYER

Client: DENVER MAGAZINE

15

Artist: **QUANG HO**

Art Director: NAOMI TRUJILLO

Client: DISCIPLESHIP JOURNAL

16

Artist: **BILL VUKSANOVICH**

Art Director: PAMELA BERRY

Client: ESQUIRE

ILLUSTRATORS31

17

Artist: **SHARON ROY FINCH**

Art Director: KIM MULLER-THYM

Client: BALTIMORE JEWISH TIMES

18

Artist: **GEOFFREY MOSS**

Art Director: ALICE DEGENHARDT

Client: CREATIVE LIVING MAGAZINE

19

Artist: **DAVID NOYES**

Art Director: DEBORAH LOCK

Client: U.S. NEWS & WORLD
REPORT

17

18

19

20

Artist: **GARY KELLEY**

Art Director: GARY KELLEY

Client: NORTH AMERICAN REVIEW

ILLUSTRATORS31

21

Artist: **SKIP LIEPKE**

Art Director: SANDY STARR

Client: NEWTON QUARTERLY

21

22

Artist: **LELAND KLANDERMAN**

Art Director: KATHY TIMMERMAN

Client: TWIN CITIES

23

Artist: **SKIP LIEPKE**

24

Artist: **TINA LIMER**

Art Director: SANDRA DIPASQUA

Client: CONNOISSEUR

22

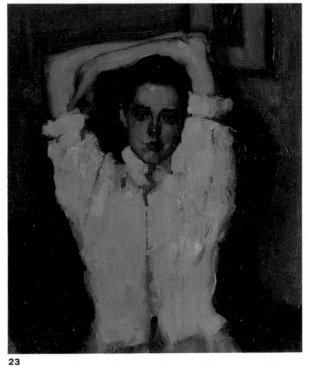

23

24

ILLUSTRATORS31

25

Artist: **JOANIE SCHWARZ**

Art Director: IRA FRIEDLANDER

Client: AMERICAN HEALTH

26

Artist: **SAMUEL BAYER**

Art Director: BASIL BERRY
              AMY SEISSLER

Client: SPIN

27

Artist: **BURT SILVERMAN**

Art Director: ROBERT BEST

Client: NEW YORK

25

26

27

28

Artist: **MARK ENGLISH**

29

Artist: **MARK WHITCOMBE**

Art Director: DANIELLE GALLO

Client: PENTHOUSE LETTERS

30

Artist: **KAREN KLUGLEIN**

Art Director: JUDY GARLAN

Client: THE ATLANTIC MONTHLY

28

29

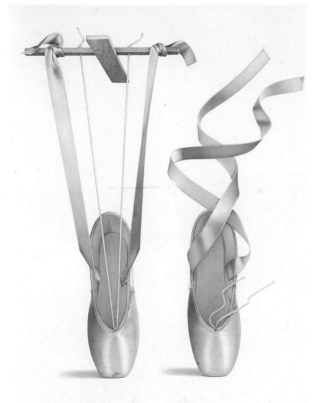

31

Artist: **KINUKO Y. CRAFT**

Art Director: TOM STAEBLER

Client: PLAYBOY

31

30

ILLUSTRATORS31

32

Artist: **BART GOLDMAN**

Art Director: LISA ORSINI

Client: MacUSER MAGAZINE

32

33

34

35

33

Artist: **DEBRA WHITE**

Art Director: PETER DEUTSCH

Client: QUALITY REVIEW

34

Artist: **DEBRA WHITE**

Art Director: PETER DEUTSCH

Client: QUALITY REVIEW

35

Artist: **BARRON STOREY**

Art Director: JANE PALECEK

Client: HIPPOCRATES

36

Artist: **MARK ENGLISH**

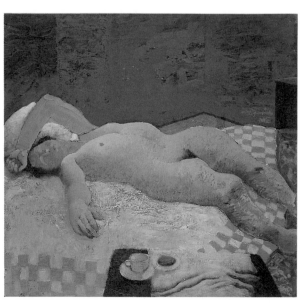

36

37

Artist: **TIM O'BRIEN**

Art Director: DAWN ROMANO

Client: NEW JERSEY MONTHLY

38

Artist: **ROBERT G. STEELE**

39

Artist: **PETER M. FIORE**

Art Director: TINA ADAMEK

Client: POSTGRADUATE MEDICINE

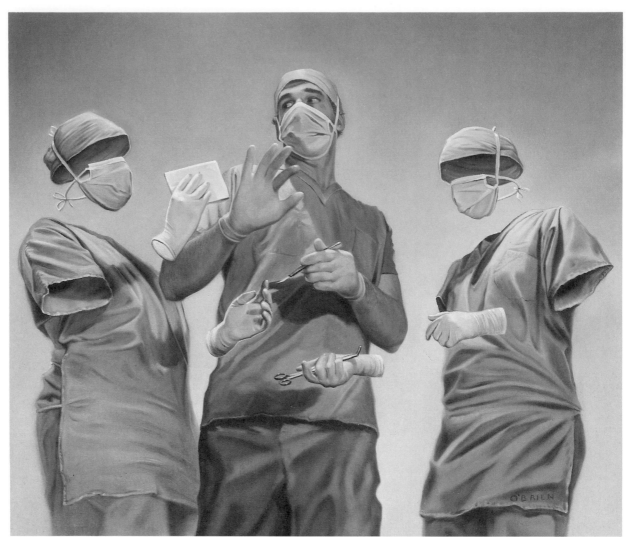

37

38

39

40

41

40

Artist: **MANGAL**

Art Director: EVERETT HALVORSEN
ROBERT MANSFIELD

Client: FORBES

41

Artist: **MANGAL**

Art Director: EVERETT HALVORSEN
RONDA KASS

Client: FORBES

42

Artist: **ELLEN THOMPSON**

Art Director: KEN PALUMBO

Client: PLAYGIRL

42

ILLUSTRATORS31

43

Artist: **CAROL WALD**

Art Director: MICHAEL BAN

Client: DETROIT MONTHLY

44

Artist: **GOTTFRIED HELNWEIN**

Art Director: ROBERT BEST

Client: NEW YORK

45

Artist: **ROBERT WISNEWSKI**

Art Director: ANNE DuVIVIER

Client: PSYCHOLOGY TODAY

43

44

45

46

48

49

46

Artist: **HARVEY DINNERSTEIN**

Art Director: ROBERT FILLIE

Client: AMERICAN ARTIST

47

Artist: **GREG SPALENKA**

Art Director: BAMBI NICKLEN

Client: WEST

48

Artist: **JOANIE SCHWARZ**

Art Director: AUDREY RAZGAITIS

Client: THE NEW YORK TIMES
        MAGAZINE

49

Artist: **DOUG GRISWOLD**

Art Director: BOB REYNOLDS

Client: SAN JOSE MERCURY NEWS

50

Artist: **KRISTEN FUNKHOUSER**

Art Director: MICHAEL WALTERS

Client: CALIFORNIA BUSINESS

51

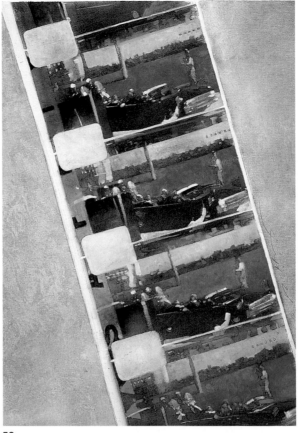

52

53

54

51

Artist: **BURT SILVERMAN**

Art Director: JOHN BELKNAP

Client: 7 DAYS

52

Artist: **ROBERT HUNT**

Art Director: LISA WRIGLEY

Client: K.C.E.T. MAGAZINE

53

Artist: **ROBERT ANDREW PARKER**

Art Director: JOAN FERRELL

Client: TRAVEL AND LEISURE

54

Artist: **JEFFREY SMITH**

Art Director: STEVE HOFFMAN

Client: NEW YORK UNIVERSITY
MAGAZINE

ILLUSTRATORS31

55

Artist: **MICHAEL PARASKEVAS**

Art Director: MICHAEL WALSH

Client: THE WASHINGTON POST

56

Artist: **MICHEL GUIRE VAKA**

Art Director: TOM STAEBLER

Client: PLAYBOY

57

Artist: **MICHEL GUIRE VAKA**

Art Director: TOM STAEBLER

Client: PLAYBOY

55

56

57

58

59

58

Artist: **DAVID LESH**

Art Director: KAY HARTMANN

Client: CHICAGO BAR ASSOCIATION

59

Artist: **DAVID LESH**

Art Director: KAY HARTMANN

Client: CHICAGO BAR ASSOCIATION

60

Artist: **GARY LANCELLE**

Art Director: ROY VALITCHKA

Client: GREEN BAY PRESS GAZETTE

60

ILLUSTRATORS**31**

61

Artist: **JIM DEAL**

Art Director: ANN WEBER
ROGER DOWD

Client: MEDICAL ECONOMICS

62

Artist: **KINUKO Y. CRAFT**

Art Director: RICHARD WEIGARD

Client: THE NEW YORK TIMES
MAGAZINE

63

Artist: **DAVID NOYES**

Art Director: DAVID NOYES

Client: INSIDE MAGAZINE

64

Artist: **THEO RUDNAK**

Art Director: GARY BERNLOEHR

Client: GEORGIA TREND

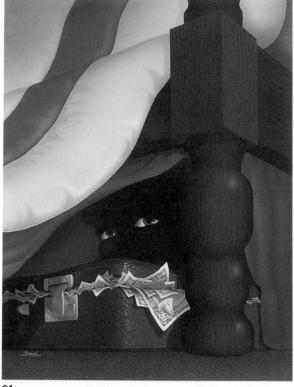

61

62

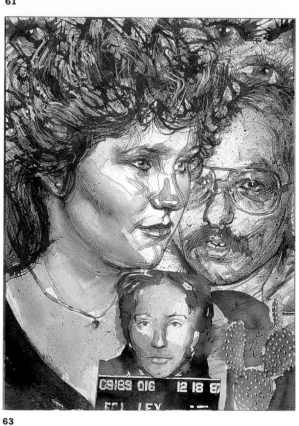

63

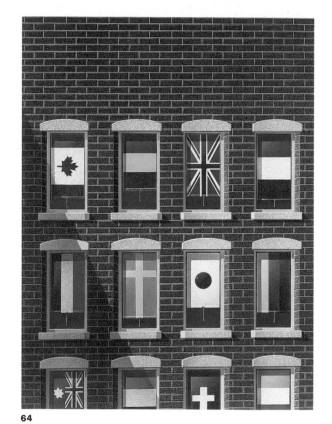

64

65

Artist: **ROBERT GIUSTI**

Art Director: TOM STAEBLER

Client: PLAYBOY

ILLUSTRATORS31

66

Artist: **WILSON McLEAN**

Art Director: RUDY HOGLUND

Client: TIME

66

67

68

69

70

67

Artist: **DANIEL SCHWARTZ**

Art Director: RUDY HOGLUND

Client: TIME

68

Artist: **C.F. PAYNE**

Art Director: D.J. STOUT

Client: TEXAS MONTHLY

69

Artist: **SALLY WERN COMPORT**

Art Director: NANCY CAHNERS

Client: M.I.T. TECHNOLOGY REVIEW

70

Artist: **WILSON McLEAN**

Art Director: ALEXANDER ISLEY

Client: SPY MAGAZINE

71

Artist: **C.F. PAYNE**

Art Director: KERRY TREMAIN

Client: MOTHER JONES

72

Artist: **DOUG GRISWOLD**

Art Director: BOB REYNOLDS

Client: SAN JOSE MERCURY NEWS

73

Artist: **NICK BACKES**

Art Director: TOM STAEBLER

Client: PLAYBOY

71

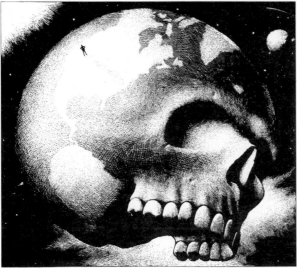

72

73

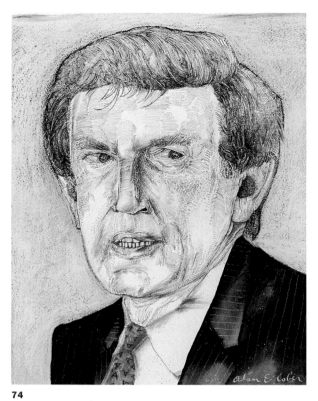

74

75

74

Artist: **ALAN E. COBER**

Art Director: FRED WOODWARD

Client: ROLLING STONE

75

Artist: **SCOTT KRISTOFF**

Art Director: MARK COLLINS

Client: NEC WORLD SERIES OF
GOLF

76

Artist: **BILL NELSON**

Art Director: LYNN HAZLEWOOD

Client: MANHATTAN, INC.

76

ILLUSTRATORS31

77

Artist: **MARVIN MATTELSON**

Art Director: RICHARD BLEIWEISS

Client: PENTHOUSE

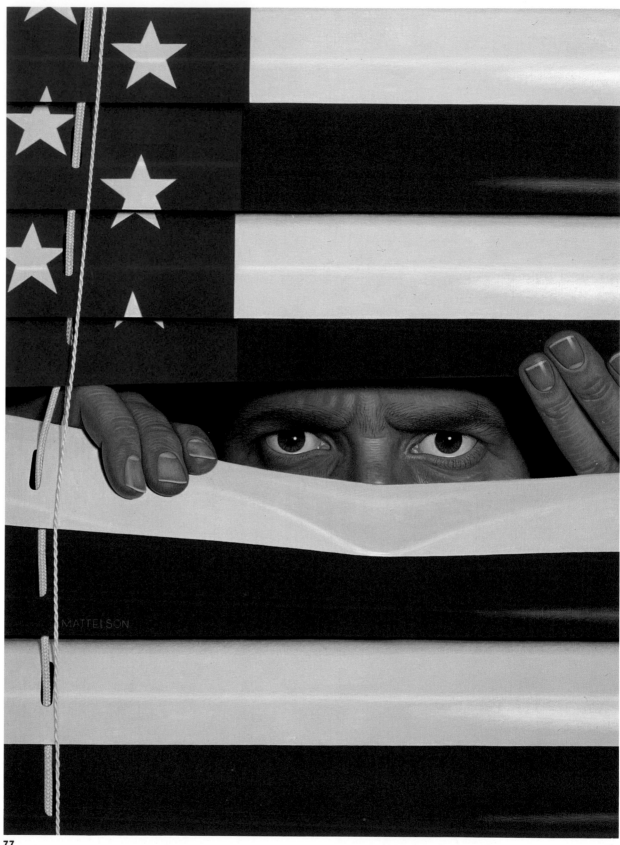

78

79

80

78

Artist: **CHRISTOPHER ZACHAROW**

Art Director: CYNTHIA FRIEDMAN

Client: BUSINESS MONTH

79

Artist: **C.F. PAYNE**

Art Director: RIP GEORGES

Client: REGARDIE'S

80

Artist: **WILSON McLEAN**

Art Director: RICHARD BLEIWEISS

Client: PENTHOUSE

ILLUSTRATORS31

81

Artist: **BRAD HOLLAND**

Art Director: HANS-GEORG
POSPISCHIL

Client: FRANKFURTER ALLGEMEINE
MAGAZIN

82

Artist: **MICHAEL PARASKEVAS**

Art Director: MICHAEL WALSH

Client: THE WASHINGTON POST

83

Artist: **BRAD HOLLAND**

Art Director: HANS-GEORG
POSPISCHIL

Client: FRANKFURTER ALLGEMEINE
MAGAZIN

81

82

83

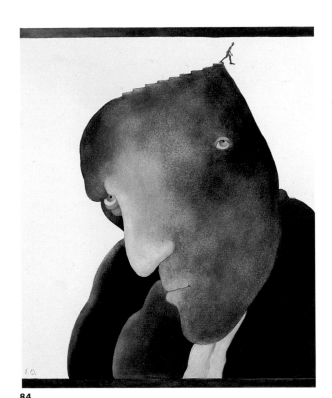

84

85

86

84

Artist: **ETIENNE DELESSERT**

Art Director: NATHALIE NATH

Client: EMOIS

85

Artist: **EDWARD SOREL**

Art Director: JUDY GARLAN

Client: THE ATLANTIC MONTHLY

86

Artist: **BRAD HOLLAND**

Art Director: HANS-GEORG
POSPISCHIL

Client: FRANKFURTER ALLGEMEINE
MAGAZIN

ILLUSTRATORS31

87

Artist: **WILLIAM LOW**

Art Director: DEBORA E. CLARK

Client: MONEY MAKER

88

Artist: **WILLIAM A. MOTTA**

Art Director: WILLIAM A. MOTTA

Client: ROAD & TRACK

89

Artist: **GUY BILLOUT**

Art Director: JUDY GARLAN

Client: THE ATLANTIC MONTHLY

87

88

89

90

91

92

90

Artist: **GUY BILLOUT**

Art Director: JUDY GARLAN

Client: THE ATLANTIC MONTHLY

91

Artist: **GUY BILLOUT**

Art Director: JUDY GARLAN

Client: THE ATLANTIC MONTHLY

92

Artist: **WILLIAM LOW**

Art Director: IRWIN GLUSKER

Client: GOURMET

93

Artist: **ROBERT GIUSTI**

Art Director: TOM STAEBLER

Client: PLAYBOY

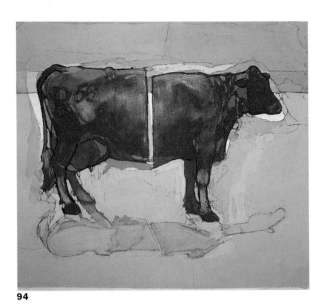

94

95

96

97

94

Artist: **JEFF MEYER**

Art Director: GREGORY CHAMBERS

Client: VEGETARIAN LIFE AND
TIMES

95

Artist: **JAN PERKINS**

Art Director: DON WELLER

Client: THE LONESTAR MAGAZINE

96

Artist: **MARK SMOLLIN**

Art Director: JILL PFEIFFER

Client: MONSANTO MAGAZINE

97

Artist: **LARS JUSTINEN**

Art Director: ED GUTHERO
LARS JUSTINEN

Client: PACIFIC PRESS

98

Artist: **ROBERT HYNES**

Art Director: URSULA VOSSELLER

Client: NATIONAL GEOGRAPHIC

99

Artist: **MIKE HODGES**

Art Director: MARYANN B. COLLINS

Client: VIRGINIA BUSINESS
MAGAZINE

100

Artist: **HORACIO FIDEL CARDO**

Art Director: JUDY ANDERSON

Client: THE CHICAGO TRIBUNE

98

99

100

101

Artist: **MARSHALL ARISMAN**

Art Director: DEBORA E. CLARK

Client: MONEY MAKER

ILLUSTRATORS31

102

Artist: **DON VANDERBEEK**

Art Director: DON REYNOLDS

Client: DAYTON NEWS

103

Artist: **ANN NEUMANN**

Art Director: JEANNE DeMATA
LIBBY MAMMAND

Client: BURROUGHS WELLCOME CO.

104

Artist: **ROBERT GIUSTI**

Art Director: TOM STAEBLER

Client: PLAYBOY

102

103

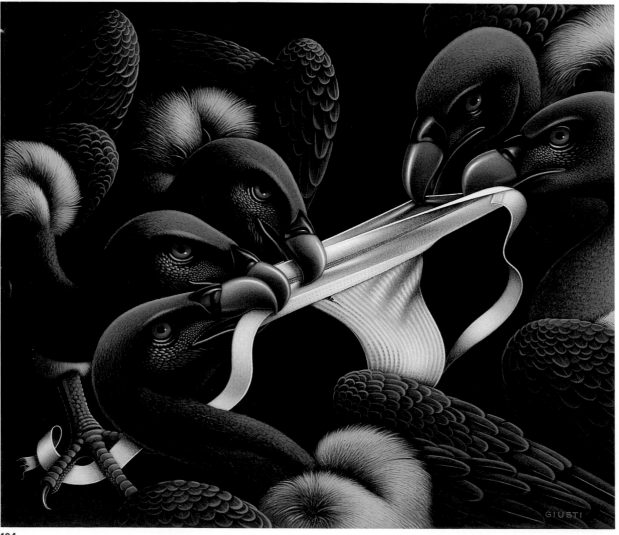

104

105

Artist: **THEO RUDNAK**

Art Director: D.J. STOUT

Client: TEXAS MONTHLY

ILLUSTRATORS31

106

Artist: **GLENN HARRINGTON**

Art Director: TINA ADAMEK

Client: POSTGRADUATE MEDICINE

107

Artist: **DAVID GROVE**

Art Director: BARRON STOREY

Client: WATCH MAGAZINE

108

Artist: **ROY PENDLETON**

Art Director: LEN WILLIS

Client: PLAYBOY

109

Artist: **GREG SPALENKA**

Art Director: GARY SLUZEWSKI

Client: CLEVELAND MAGAZINE

106

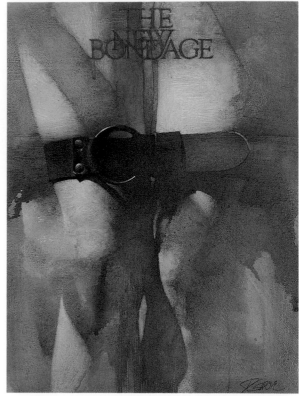

107

108

109

ILLUSTRATORS**31**

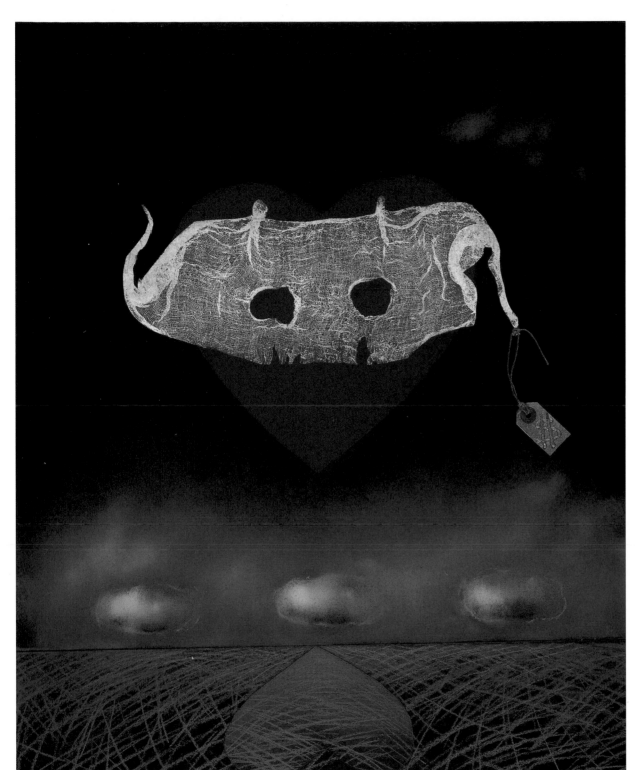

110

Artist: **SANDRA FILIPPUCCI**

Art Director: TINA ADAMEK

Client: GRAFICA MAGAZINE

ILLUSTRATORS31

111

Artist: **JEFFREY SMITH**

Art Director: PATRICIA BRADBURY

Client: NEWSWEEK

112

Artist: **ROB CORSETTI**

Art Director: LISA HILDEBRANDT

Client: NOVELL

113

Artist: **WILLIAM LOW**

Art Director: IRWIN GLUSKER

Client: GOURMET

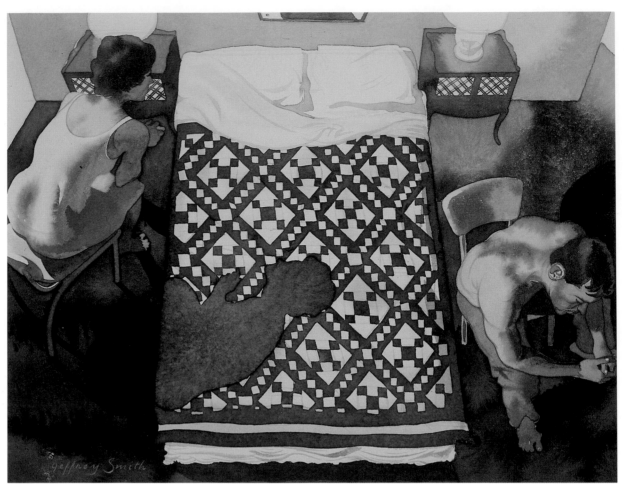

111

112

113

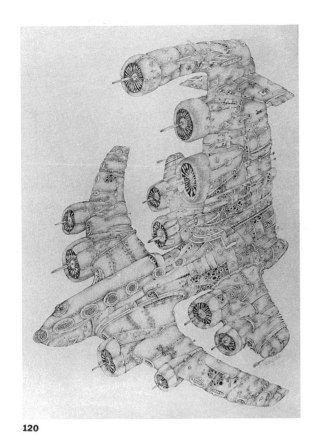

120

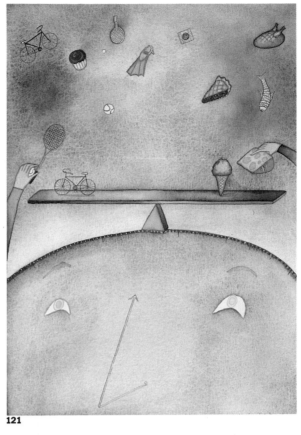

121

122

123

120

Artist: **JIM SPANFELLER**

Art Director: MIRIAM SMITH

Client: NEWSDAY

121

Artist: **LONNI SUE JOHNSON**

Art Director: TINA ADAMEK

Client: POSTGRADUATE MEDICINE

122

Artist: **ETIENNE DELESSERT**

Art Director: NATHALIE NATH

Client: EMOIS

123

Artist: **ETIENNE DELESSERT**

Art Director: NATHALIE NATH

Client: EMOIS

ILLUSTRATORS31

124

Artist: **MAX GINSBURG**

Art Director: ROBERT BEST

Client: NEW YORK

125

Artist: **DAVID WEBB**

Art Director: SUSAN WALDRIP
DENDY

Client: COOKING LIGHT

124

125

126

Artist: **RAFAL OLBINSKI**

Art Director: JERELLE KRAUS

Client: THE NEW YORK TIMES

ILLUSTRATORS31

127

Artist: **RICHARD FISH**

Art Director: JUDY GARLAN

Client: THE ATLANTIC MONTHLY

128

Artist: **STANLEY MELTZOFF**

Art Director: VICTOR CLOSI

Client: FIELD & STREAM

129

Artist: **STANLEY MELTZOFF**

Art Director: VICTOR CLOSI

Client: FIELD & STREAM

127

128

129

130

131

132

133

Artist: **WILLIAM V. CIGLIANO**

Art Director: KATHY KELLEY

Client: CHICAGO

134

Artist: **WALT SPITZMILLER**

Art Director: JERRY ALTEN

Client: TV GUIDE

135

Artist: **LANE SMITH**

Art Director: ROSSLYN A. FRICK

Client: AMIGA WORLD

136

Artist: **FRANCIS LIVINGSTON**

Art Director: CHUCK DONALD

Client: SACRAMENTO MAGAZINE

133

134

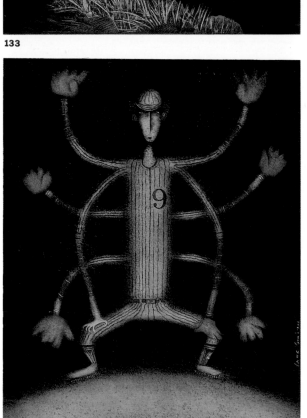

135

136

137

Artist: **MARVIN MATTELSON**

Art Director: RICHARD BLEIWEISS

Client: PENTHOUSE

ILLUSTRATORS31

138

Artist: **FRED OTNES**

Art Director: HOWARD E. PAINE

Client: NATIONAL GEOGRAPHIC

139

Artist: **FRED OTNES**

Art Director: HOWARD E. PAINE

Client: NATIONAL GEOGRAPHIC

140

Artist: **FRED OTNES**

Art Director: HOWARD E. PAINE

Client: NATIONAL GEOGRAPHIC

138

139

140

141

142

143

141

Artist: **BILL FARNSWORTH**

142

Artist: **JOHN BERKEY**

Art Director: J. ROBERT TERINGO

Client: NATIONAL GEOGRAPHIC

143

Artist: **GEOFFREY MOSS**

Art Director: GARY BERNLOEHR

Client: GEORGIA TREND

AWARD WINNERS

JURY

BLAIR DRAWSON
GOLD MEDAL

ETIENNE DELESSERT
SILVER MEDAL

HENRIK DRESCHER
SILVER MEDAL

**WILSON McLEAN,
Chairman**
Illustrator

JANINE MAYHEW
Art Director,
Cohen, Marino & Paino

ALAN E. COBER
Illustrator/Professor,
S.U.N.Y., Buffalo

ALMA PHIPPS
Art Director,
Chief Executive Magazine

TOM CURRY
Illustrator

MILT SIMPSON
Johnson & Simpson
Graphic Designers

STEVE GUARNACCIA
Illustrator

DARRYL ZUDECK
Illustrator

DAVID LESH
Illustrator

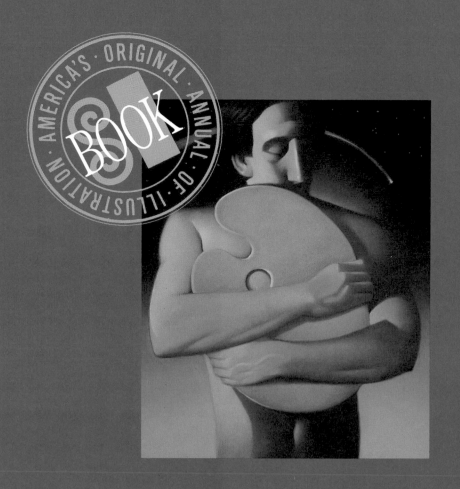

BLAIR DRAWSON

Drawson's work has appeared in children's books, record and book jackets, posters, postcards, advertising, and numerous major publications.

He also draws the comic strip *The Building*, which appears in *New York Woman*, a monthly magazine.

Drawson has lectured at Parsons School of Design, Northern Illinois University, the University of Wisconsin, and at his own alma mater, the Ontario College of Art.

Art Director: **LOUISE FILI**

Client: **PANTHEON BOOKS**

144

ETIENNE DELESSERT

Born in 1941 in Lausanne, Switzerland, Delessert is a painter, writer, graphic designer, and director of animated films.

He has illustrated more than forty books and has won numerous awards, including four Gold Medals from the Society of Illustrators.

In 1975 he was honored with a retrospective exhibition at the Louvre.

Art Director: RITA MARSHALL

Client: CREATIVE EDUCATION

ILLUSTRATORS**31**

HENRIK DRESCHER

Born in 1955 in Copenhagen, Denmark, Drescher began drawing seriously when he was 15. He did a great deal of traveling and has lived in many cities in the United States and abroad.

He prefers to work on illustration one-third of his time, children's books one-third, and note-books/painting the other third.

His big ambition in life is "to teach mosquitos to attack each other and leave us people be."

Art Director: CAROL CARSON

Client: ALFRED A. KNOPF

146

147

148

Artist: **JOHN RUSH**

Art Director: CAROL CARSON

Client: ALFRED A. KNOPF

Artist: **MARK ENGLISH**

Art Director: JIM PLUMERI

Client: BANTAM BOOKS

148

149

Artist: **MARK ENGLISH**

Art Director: JIM PLUMERI

Client: BANTAM BOOKS

149

150

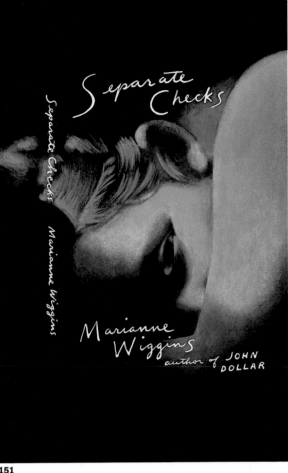

151

150

Artist: **JOSE MARZAN JR.**

151

Artist: **PAUL DAVIS**

Art Director: JOSEPH MONTEBELLO

Client: HARPER & ROW

152

Artist: **SARA SCHWARTZ**

Art Director: DAVID BULLEN

Client: NORTH POINT PRESS

153

Artist: **LANE SMITH**

Art Director: MARTHA PHILLIPS

Client: THE FRANKLIN LIBRARY

152

153

154

Artist: **JULIAN ALLEN**

Art Director: LOUISE FILI

Client: PANTHEON BOOKS

155

Artist: **HIRO KIMURA**

156

Artist: **BILL NELSON**

Art Director: LOUISE FILI

Client: PANTHEON BOOKS

154

155

156

157

158

157

Artist: **WILSON McLEAN**

158

Artist: **ETIENNE DELESSERT**

Art Director: RITA MARSHALL

Client: FARRAR STRAUS GIROUX

ILLUSTRATORS31

159

Artist: **SUSI KILGORE**

160

Artist: **RICHARD MANTEL**

Art Director: ROBERT REED

Client: HENRY HOLT & CO.

161

Artist: **ANDRZEJ DUDZINSKI**

Art Director: LOUISE FILI

Client: PANTHEON BOOKS

162

Artist: **MEL ODOM**

Art Director: VICTOR WEAVER

Client: DELL PUBLISHING

159

160

161

162

163

163

Artist: **JOHN JINKS**

Art Director: JIM PLUMERI

Client: BANTAM BOOKS

164

Artist: **MARK PENBERTHY**

Art Director: MARTHA PHILLIPS

Client: THE FRANKLIN LIBRARY

165

Artist: **ERIC DINYER**

Art Director: CHRISTINE FOEDERER

164

165

166

Artist: **KENT WILLIAMS**

Art Director: ARCHIE GOODWIN
 DANIEL CHICHESTER

Client: EPIC

167

168

169

167

Artist: **WAYNE BARLOWE**

Art Director: DON PUCKEY

Client: WARNER BOOKS

168

Artist: **ROBERT GOLDSTROM**

Art Director: ALEX GOTFRYD

Client: DOUBLEDAY

169

Artist: **BASCOVE**

Art Director: NEIL STUART

Client: VIKING PENGUIN

170

Artist: **JAMES STEINBERG**

Art Director: JOSEPH MONTEBELLO

Client: HARPER & ROW

171

Artist: **STEPHEN PERINGER**

Art Director: BARBARA BUCK

Client: WARNER BOOKS

172

Artist: **JAVIER ROMERO**

Art Director: ALEX JAY
RANDALL REICH

Client: BYRON PREISS VISUAL
PUBLICATIONS

170

171

172

173

Artist: **WENDELL MINOR**

Art Director: AL CETTA

Client: T.Y. CROWELL

174

Artist: **WENDELL MINOR**

Art Director: CINDY SIMON

Client: LOTHROP LEE & SHEPARD

173

174

ILLUSTRATORS**31**

175

Artist: **TERESA FASOLINO**

Art Director: J.C. SUARÈS

Client: PRENTICE-HALL

175

176

177

178

176
Artist: **MICHAEL PARASKEVAS**

177
Artist: **RICHARD ROSS**

Art Director: BARBARA BUCK

Client: WARNER BOOKS

178
Artist: **TOM SCIACCA**

Art Director: ROBIN
GILMORE-BARNES

Client: BANTAM BOOKS

179

Artist: **ISADORE SELTZER**

Art Director: MARTIN SOLOMON

Client: ROYAL COMPOSING ROOM

180

Artist: **DAVE CALVER**

Art Director: SUSAN MITCHELL

Client: VINTAGE

181

Artist: **ISADORE SELTZER**

Art Director: MARTIN SOLOMON

Client: ROYAL COMPOSING ROOM

182

Artist: **ISADORE SELTZER**

Art Director: MARTIN SOLOMON

Client: ROYAL COMPOSING ROOM

179

180

181

182

183

Artist: **JOHN KLEBER**

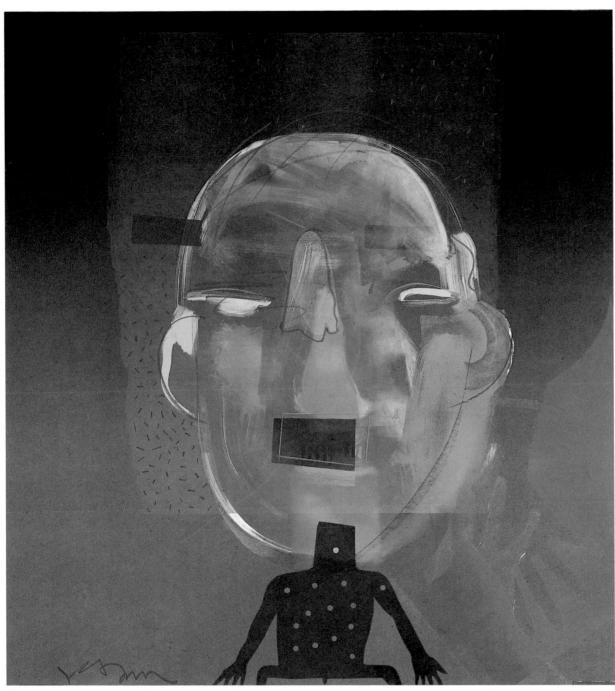

183

ILLUSTRATORS31

184

Artist: **THEO RUDNAK**

Art Director: JEANNIE FRIEDMAN
ELLIOT KRELOFF

Client: SILVER BURDETT
& GINN

185

Artist: **FRED MARCELLINO**

Art Director: ALEX GOTFRYD

Client: DOUBLEDAY

186

Artist: **ROBERT ANDREW PARKER**

Art Director: LOUISE FILI

Client: PANTHEON BOOKS

184

185

186

187

188

187

Artist: **FRED MARCELLINO**

Art Director: JOSEPH MONTEBELLO

Client: HARPER & ROW

188

Artist: **MICHELLE BARNES**

Art Director: SARA EISENMAN

Client: HOUGHTON MIFFLIN

189

Artist: **MARK HESS**

Art Director: BARBARA BUCK

Client: WARNER BOOKS

189

190

191

192

190

Artist: **GARY KELLEY**

Art Director: MARY SIEGEL

Client: NEW AMERICAN LIBRARY

191

Artist: **CHERYL GRIESBACH
STANLEY MARTUCCI**

Art Director: TOM EGNER

Client: AVON BOOKS

192

Artist: **ROBERT CRAWFORD**

Art Director: JACKIE MERRI MEYER

Client: WARNER BOOKS

193

Artist: **RAPHAEL & BOLOGNESE**

Art Director: NEIL STUART

Client: VIKING PENGUIN

194

Artist: **EDWARD S. GAZSI**

Art Director: FRAN NIMECK

Client: MIDDLESEX COUNTY
HERITAGE & CULTURAL
COMMITTEE

195

Artist: **TOM HALLMAN**

Art Director: JIM PLUMERI

Client: BANTAM BOOKS

193

194

195

196

Artist: **DOUGLAS SMITH**

Art Director: SARA EISENMAN

Client: HOUGHTON MIFFLIN

197

Artist: **KINUKO Y. KRAFT**

Art Director: KIT HINRICHS

Client: CHRONICLE BOOKS

198

Artist: **TERRY WIDENER**

Art Director: BRUCE HALL
PATTI ESLINGER

Client: POCKET BOOKS

199

Artist: **TERRY WIDENER**

Art Director: MARTHA PHILLIPS

Client: THE FRANKLIN LIBRARY

197

198

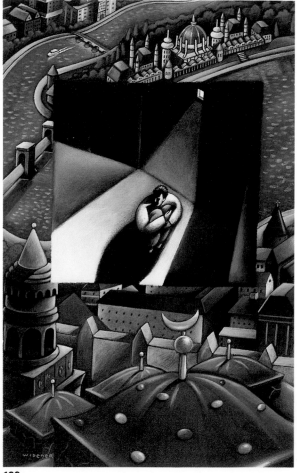

199

200

Artist: **HIRO KIMURA**

201

Artist: **PHILLIPE WEISBECKER**

Art Director: JOSEPH MONTEBELLO

Client: HARPER & ROW

202

Artist: **MARSHALL ARISMAN**

Art Director: GENE MYDLOWSKI

Client: BERKLEY BOOKS

203

Artist: **MARSHALL ARISMAN**

Art Director: GENE MYDLOWSKI

Client: BERKLEY BOOKS

201

202

203

204

205

206

204

Artist: **KEITH BAKER**

Art Director: JOY CHU

Client: HARCOURT BRACE
JOVANOVICH

205

Artist: **JOHN H. HOWARD**

Art Director: VAUGHN ANDREWS

Client: HARCOURT BRACE
JOVANOVICH

206

Artist: **JOHN H. HOWARD**

Art Director: MARY SIEGAL

Client: NEW AMERICAN LIBRARY

207

Artist: **MARVIN MATTELSON**

Art Director: SILAS RHODES

Client: SCHOOL OF VISUAL ARTS

207

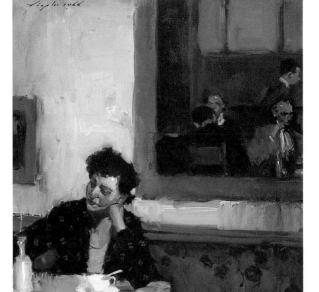

208

209

208

Artist: **SKIP LIEPKE**

209

Artist: **JANE COWLEY SZWED**

210

Artist: **SKIP LIEPKE**

210

ILLUSTRATORS31

211

Artist: **VICTORIA LOWE**

Art Director: VICTORIA LOWE

Client: P.A.J. PUBLICATIONS

212

Artist: **MICHAEL PARASKEVAS**

211

WARREN EVERETT QUIST ATTEMPTS TO LEAP INTO ANOTHER GLASS OF WATER

212

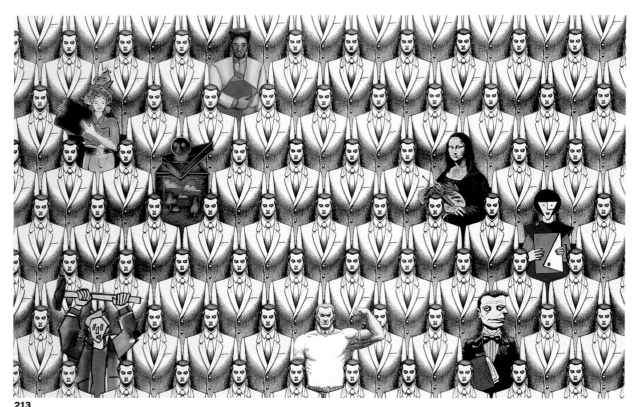

213

213

Artist: **MIRKO ILIĆ**
NICKY LINDEMAN

Art Director: WALTER BERNARD
MILTON GLASER

Client: MADISON SQUARE PRESS

214

Artist: **GREG RAGLAND**

Art Director: JOSEPH MONTEBELLO

Client: HARPER & ROW

215

Artist: **PAUL MICICH**

Art Director: DENNIS CLARK
RANDY MESSER

Client: PERFECTION FORM CO.

214

215

216

Artist: **ERIC FOWLER**

Art Director: JOSEPH MONTEBELLO

Client: HARPER & ROW

217

Artist: **STEVE JOHNSON**

Art Director: MARTHA PHILLIPS

Client: THE FRANKLIN LIBRARY

216

217

218

Artist: **DANIEL TORRES**

Art Director: MELISSA JACOBY

Client: VIKING PENGUIN

219

Artist: **FRANK GARGIULO**

220

Artist: **LISA DESIMINI**

Art Director: TONI MARKIET

Client: HARPER & ROW

219

220

221

223

221

Artist: **FRANK GARGIULO**

222

Artist: **JOHN JINKS**

Art Director: KRYSTYNA SKALSKI

Client: BANTAM BOOKS

223

Artist: **EDWARD SOREL**

Art Director: CYNTHIA KRUPAT

Client: HILL AND WANG

222

224

Artist: **KENT WILLIAMS**

Art Director: ARCHIE GOODWIN

Client: EPIC

225

Artist: **DAVID SHANNON**

Art Director: LOUISE FILI

Client: PANTHEON BOOKS

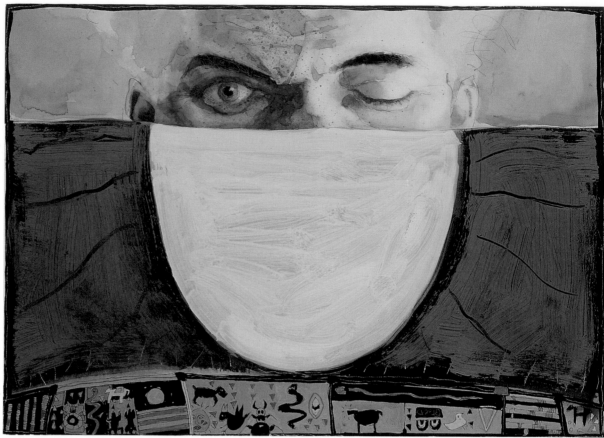

224

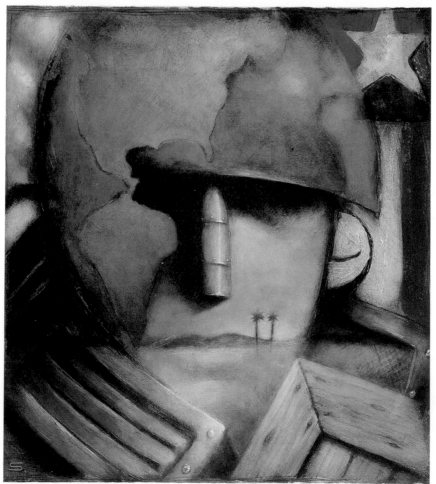

225

226

226

Artist: **TERRANCE CUMMINGS**

Art Director: SUSAN MITCHELL

Client: VINTAGE

227

Artist: **MARVIN MATTELSON**

Art Director: GEORGE CORNELL

Client: NEW AMERICAN LIBRARY

228

Artist: **M. JOHN ENGLISH**

Client: SILVER BURDETT & GINN

227

228

ILLUSTRATORS31

229

Artist: **PETER DE SÈVE**

Art Director: KELLY LYNN

Client: RANDOM HOUSE

230

Artist: **GREG RAGLAND**

Art Director: JOSEPH MONTEBELLO

Client: HARPER & ROW

231

Artist: **KAM MAK**

Art Director: BARBARA BUCK

Client: WARNER BOOKS

229

230

231

232

Artist: **JAMES McMULLAN**

Art Director: LOUISE FILI

Client: PANTHEON BOOKS

233

Artist: **JAMES MARSH**

Art Director: SARA EISENMAN

Client: HOUGHTON MIFFLIN

234

Artist: **THOMAS WOODRUFF**

Art Director: CAROL CARSON

Client: ALFRED A. KNOPF

235

Artist: **DOUGLAS FRASER**

Art Director: SARA EISENMAN

Client: HOUGHTON MIFFLIN

233

234

235

236

Artist: **WENDELL MINOR**

Art Director: JACKIE MERRI MEYER

Client: WARNER BOOKS

236

237

Artist: **ETIENNE DELESSERT**

Art Director: RITA MARSHALL

Client: FARRAR STRAUS GIROUX

238

Artist: **JOE CIARDIELLO**

Art Director: DOROTHY SCHMIDT
DAVE TROOPER

Client: READER'S DIGEST BOOKS

239

Artist: **JOE CIARDIELLO**

Art Director: DOROTHY SCHMIDT
DAVE TROOPER

Client: READER'S DIGEST BOOKS

237

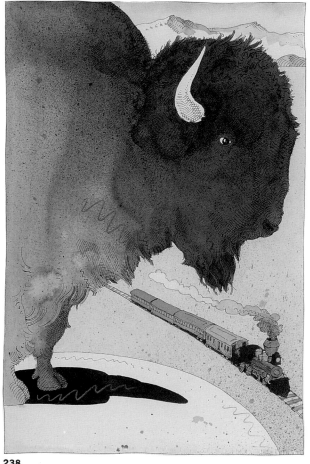

238

239

240

240

Artist: **MARK PENBERTHY**

Art Director: ROBIN SCHIFF

Client: ATLANTIC MONTHLY PRESS

241

Artist: **WALTON FORD**

Art Director: CAROL CARSON

Client: ALFRED A. KNOPF

242

Artist: **AMY HILL**

Art Director: MELISSA JACOBY

Client: VIKING PENGUIN

241

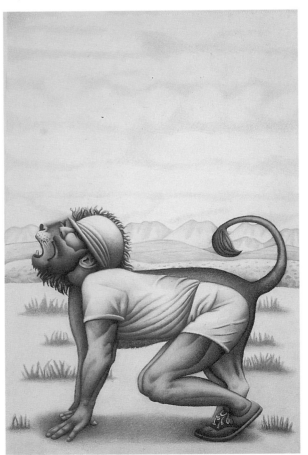

242

243

Artist: **ALAIN GAUTHIER**

Art Director: NEIL STUART

Client: VIKING PENGUIN

244

Artist: **JOHN JUDE PALENCAR**

Art Director: GENE MYDLOWSKI

Client: BERKLEY BOOKS

245

Artist: **ED YOUNG**

Art Director: NANETTE STEVENSON

Client: PUTNAM & GROSSET GROUP

243

244

245

246

Artist: **HIRO KIMURA**

Art Director: VICTOR WEAVER

Client: DELL PUBLISHING

247

Artist: **LEO LIONNI**

Art Director: DENISE CRONIN

Client: ALFRED A. KNOPF

246

247

248

Artist: **JERRY PINKNEY**

Art Director: ATHA TEHON

Client: DIAL BOOKS

249

Artist: **TROY HOWELL**

Art Director: NANETTE STEVENSON

Client: PUTNAM & GROSSET GROUP

248

249

250

251

252

253

250

Artist: **DAVID FRAMPTON**

Art Director: ROBERT D.
SCUDELLARI

Client: ALFRED A. KNOPF

251

Artist: **MARK BEYER**

Art Director: FRANCOISE
MOULY
ART SPIEGELMAN

Client: PANTHEON BOOKS

252

Artist: **MARYJANE BEGIN**

Art Director: ELLEN FRIEDMAN

Client: WILLIAM MORROW

253

Artist: **MARYJANE BEGIN**

Art Director: ELLEN FRIEDMAN

Client: WILLIAM MORROW

254

Artist: **CHARLES SANTORE**

Art Director: DON BENDER

Client: JELLYBEAN PRESS

254

255

256

255

Artist: **CHARLES SANTORE**

Art Director: DON BENDER

Client: JELLYBEAN PRESS

256

Artist: **CHARLES SANTORE**

Art Director: DON BENDER

Client: JELLYBEAN PRESS

AWARD WINNERS

MIRKO ILIĆ
GOLD MEDAL

DANIEL CRAIG
SILVER MEDAL

ROBERT GIUSTI
SILVER MEDAL

EUGENE HOFFMAN
SILVER MEDAL

JURY

**NAIAD EINSEL,
Chairman**
Illustrator

MAX GINSBERG
Illustrator

TINA ADAMEK
Executive Art Director,
Postgraduate Medicine

DAVID SHANNON
Illustrator

RICHARD BERENSON
Art Director, *Reader's Digest*

DOUGLAS SMITH
Illustrator

NICK GAETANO
Illustrator

MURRAY TINKELMAN
Illustrator/Professor,
Syracuse University

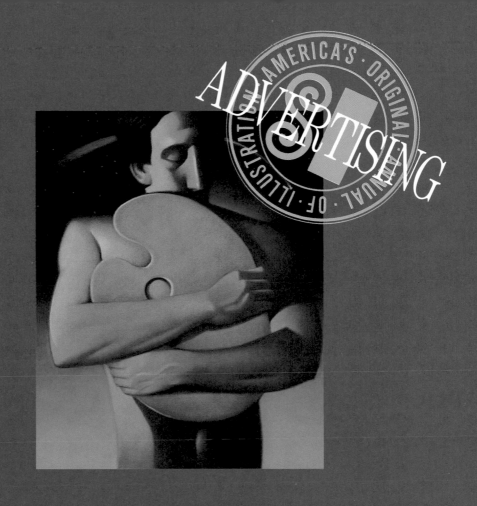

MIRKO ILIĆ

Born in Yugoslavia, Ilić's career began there at the age of seventeen. His work ranged from comics and illustrations to art direction and design for film and theater posters, album covers and books. Eventually his work was published throughout Europe.

Since his recent move to the United States his clients include *Time, US News, The New York Times, The Los Angeles Times, The Wall Street Journal,* Random House, WBMG, and Pentagram Design.

Client: **YUGOSLAV PRESS AND CULTURAL CENTER**

257

258

DANIEL CRAIG

Born in 1957 in Mankato, Minnesota, Craig received his art education at the Minneapolis College of Art and Design. Playing the violin in a bluegrass band helped put him through art school.

He graduated in 1980 and through an association with three other artists created Oasis Art Studio, a successful illustration studio located in Minneapolis.

He lives a short commute away in Saint Paul with his wife and two children.

Art Director: **BOB UPTON**

Agency: **DESIGNED MARKETING**

Client: **MINNESOTA ZOOLOGICAL GARDENS**

ROBERT GIUSTI

Born in Zurich, Switzerland, Giusti was raised in New York City. After graduating from Cranbrook Academy of Art in Michigan he began working in New York City as a graphic designer and art director. He also taught illustration at the School of Visual Arts.

The recipient of many awards, Giusti now lives in New Milford, Connecticut, with his wife, Grace, and their dog, Olive, surrounded by nature and wildlife, his favorite subjects.

Art Director: **BOB MANLEY**

Agency: **ALTMAN & MANLEY**

Client: **FRENCH TRANSIT LTD.**

259

EUGENE HOFFMAN

Born in 1933 in Gettysburg, Pennsylvania, Hoffman was self taught in art. He began his career at a small studio in Phoenix, then freelanced in San Francisco where he discovered his bias for assemblage, collage, and bricollage.

After several years in the Bay area, he moved to Colorado, where he has lived for over 25 years, enjoying the mountains for their solitude, source of inspiration and wealth of materials.

Art Director: ANN DOUDEN

Client: DENVER MUSEUM OF NATURAL HISTORY

ILLUSTRATORS31

261

Artist: **LELAND KLANDERMAN**

Art Director: NANCY RICE

Agency: RICE AND RICE

Client: MILLIKEN CONTRACT

262

Artist: **NORMAN WALKER**

Art Director: ALAN WEINBERG

Client: CBS RECORDS

261

262

263

Artist: **EDWARD S. GAZSI**

Art Director: MYRTLE JOHNSON

Agency: C&G ADVERTISING

Client: CIBA-GEIGY

264

Artist: **JAMES McMULLAN**

Art Director: JIM RUSSEK

Agency: RUSSEK ADVERTISING

Client: LINCOLN CENTER THEATER

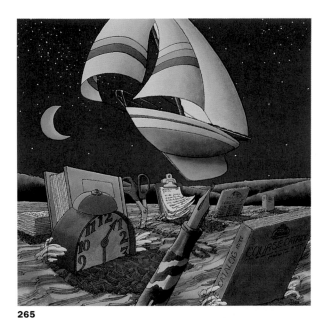

265

266

267

265

Artist: **BOB CONGE**

Art Director: BOB CONGE

Client: INFORMATION ASSOCIATES

266

Artist: **ROBERT RODRIGUEZ**

Art Director: MARCIA LERNER

Client: NEW YORK NATIONAL BOAT
SHOW

267

Artist: **ROBERT M. CUNNINGHAM**

Art Director: CRAFTON STAGG

Agency: AUSTIN KELLEY
ADVERTISING

Client: DATAW ISLAND/ALCOA
PROPERTIES

ILLUSTRATORS31

268

Artist: **LORI LOHSTOETER**

Art Director: STACY DRUMMOND

Client: CBS RECORDS

269

Artist: **WENDELL MINOR**

Art Director: AL CETTA

Client: T.Y. CROWELL

268

269

270

271

272

270

Artist: **RICHARD SPARKS**

Art Director: JERRY DEMONEY

Client: MOBIL/PBS

271

Artist: **JULIAN ALLEN**

Art Director: DREW HODGES

Agency: SPOT DESIGN

Client: ROLLING STONE

272

Artist: **PAUL CASALE**

Client: NAHAS GALLERY

273

Artist: **JOEL PETER JOHNSON**

Art Director: PAMELA GIBBS

Client: STUDIO ARENA THEATRE

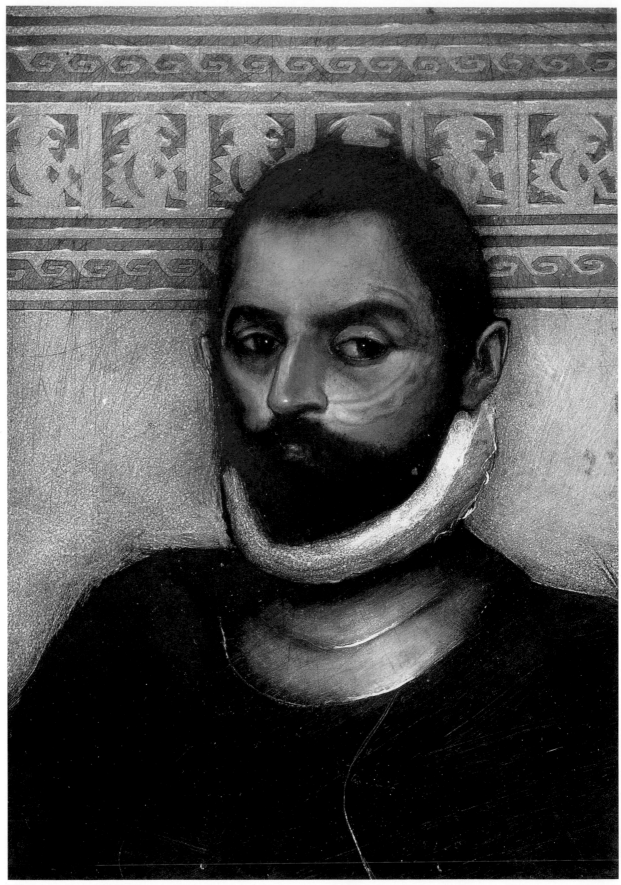

273

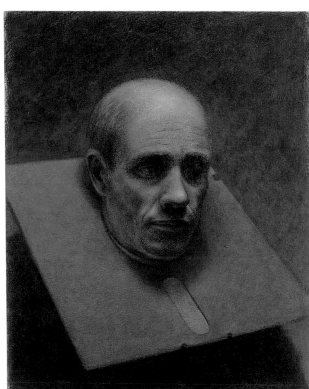

274

275

274

Artist: **MIKE HODGES**

275

Artist: **JOEL PETER JOHNSON**

Art Director: ALAN E. COBER
              KATHLEEN C. HOWELL

Client: SUNY AT BUFFALO

276

Artist: **NORMAN WALKER**

Art Director: ALAN WEINBERG

Client: CBS RECORDS

276

277

Artist: **JOHN JINKS**

Art Director: MICHAEL RANDAZZO

Agency: MICHAEL RANDAZZO
ADVERTISING

Client: KENMARK OPTICAL

278

Artist: **KEVIN BURKE**

Art Director: GRAIG TSHILDES
RAY McCORMACK

Client: MOTOROLA

279

Artist: **SUE ROTHER**

Client: NIKKO HOTEL

277

278

279

280

281

Artist: **JANE STERRETT**

Art Director: PATTY CALLAND

Agency: MELVIN SIMON

Client: HOLLYWOOD PROMENADE

281

Artist: **ANDREW PAQUETTE**

Art Director: STEVEN BYRAM

Client: CBS RECORDS

ILLUSTRATORS**31**

282

Artist: **SEYMOUR CHWAST**

Art Director: SEYMOUR CHWAST

Client: ROCKWELL INTERNATIONAL

282

283

Artist: **IVAN CHERMAYEFF**

Art Director: IVAN CHERMAYEFF

Client: GRAMAVISION

284

Artist: **STEPHEN TURK**

Art Director: TIM HARTUNG

Client: AT&T

285

Artist: **JACK MOLLOY**

Art Director: LAURA DES ENFANTS
AMY SRUBAS

Client: Y.M.C.A.

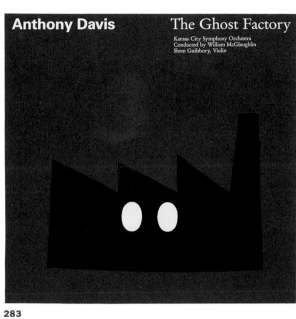

283

284

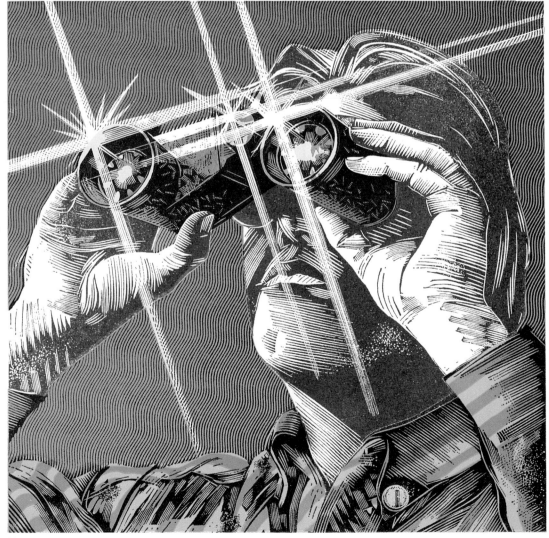

285

289

Artist: **MARK HESS**

Art Director: WOODY LOWE

Agency: HAL RINEY & PARTNERS

Client: ANHEUSER-BUSCH

289

290

Artist: **BART GOLDMAN**

Art Director: BONNIE RESNICK

Agency: ORIT DESIGN, INC.

Client: SONY VIDEO SOFTWARE

291

Artist: **ALEX EBEL**

Art Director: BILL NIRENBERG

Client: L.P.F. PUBLICATIONS

292

Artist: **GEORGE ANGELINI**

Art Director: PAUL OMIN

Client: READER'S DIGEST

290

291

292

293

Artist: **STEVE JOHNSON**

Art Director: MIKE FORNWALD

Agency: FRANKENBERRY, LAUGHLIN
AND CONSTABLE

Client: H.M. GRAPHICS

294

Artist: **ROBERT CRAWFORD**

Art Director: LOUIS DiBACCO

Agency: KEILER ADVERTISING

Client: TEXTRON/LYCOMING

293

294

295

Artist: **BILL MAYER**

Art Director: MARV KUNZE

Agency: BAUMWOLD & TANNER
ASSOCIATES

Client: DRAKE BEAM MORIN, INC.

296

Artist: **BURT SILVERMAN**

Art Director: DRENAN LINDSAY

Agency: EDDIE BAUER ADVERTISING

Client: EDDIE BAUER, INC.

297

Artist: **CYNTHIA MILLER**

Art Director: BILL JOHNSON

Client: COLUMBIA RECORDS

295

296

297

ILLUSTRATORS31

298

Artist: **THEO RUDNAK**

Art Director: BOB FEARON

Agency: FEARON/GBA

Client: NEW YORK TIMES MAGAZINE
GROUP

298

299

299

Artist: **JACK MOLLOY**

Art Director: KENT HENSLEY

Client: DAYTON HUDSON
        DEPARTMENT STORE

300

Artist: **FRANCIS LIVINGSTON**

Art Director: CHUCK STERN

Client: CALIFORNIA FIRST BANK

301

Artist: **JON FLAMING**

Art Director: RON SULLIVAN

Agency: SULLIVAN PERKINS

Client: THE ROUSE COMPANY/
        WESTLAKE CENTER

300

301

ILLUSTRATORS31

302

Artist: **LAUREN KESWICK**

Art Director: LORI JUSTICE

Agency: MAHER KAUMP & CLARK

Client: HALL PHARMACEUTICAL

303

Artist: **C. BRUCE MORSER**

Art Director: KEITH CAMPBELL

Agency: JOHN BROWN AND
PARTNERS

Client: VIRGINIA MASON HOSPITAL

304

Artist: **JOHN THOMPSON**

Art Director: STAVROS
COSMOPULOS
RICHARD KERSTEIN

Agency: COSMOPULOS, CROWLEY &
DALY

Client: ALLENDALE INSURANCE

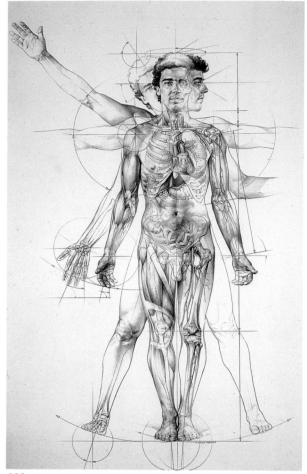

303

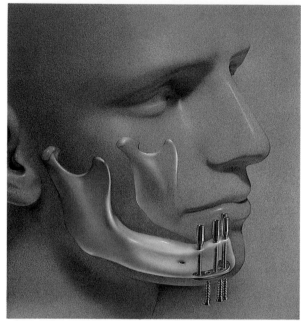

302

304

305

Artist: **ROBERT G. STEELE**

Art Director: RICK BEAULIEU

Agency: McCAFFREY &
McCALL, INC.

Client: MERCEDES-BENZ

306

Artist: **ALAN E. COBER**

Art Director: BRAD COPELAND
MAXEY ANDRESS

Client: NEENAH PAPER

307

Artist: **KAREN BARBOUR**

Art Director: RICHARD MANTEL

Client: NEW YORK

305

306

307

308

Artist: **GEORGE Y. ABE**

Art Director: JACK RAMSEY

Agency: JACK RAMSEY
ADVERTISING

Client: INTEL CORPORATION

309

Artist: **JAMES TUGHAN**

Art Director: MIKE SHERFIN

Agency: JORDAN, McGRATH, CASE

Client: AETNA

310

Artist: **MARK PENBERTHY**

Art Director: CHARLES ROUTHIER
CLEMENT MOK

Client: FARALLON COMPANY

308

309

310

311

Artist: **GEORGE Y. ABE**

Art Director: JACK RAMSEY

Agency: JACK RAMSEY
ADVERTISING

Client: INTEL CORPORATION

312

Artist: **KATHERINE MAHONEY**

Art Director: BETH MAYER CARLISLE
PAUL BALDISSINNI

Client: PERSONICS

311

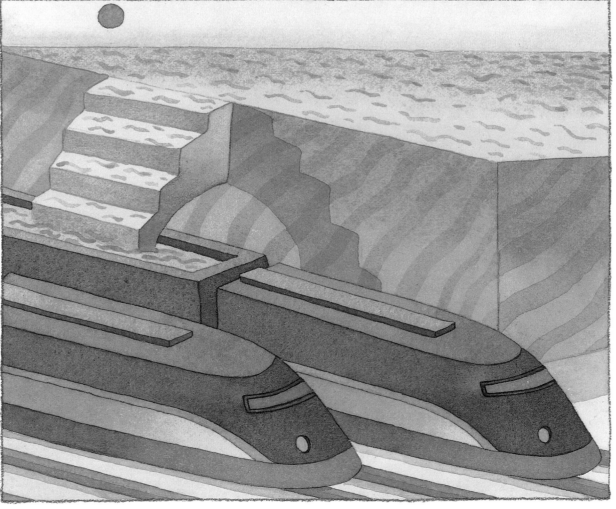

312

ILLUSTRATORS31

313

Artist: **GARY KELLEY**

Art Director: WILLIAM HOSNER

Client: CENTER FOR CREATIVE
STUDIES

314

Artist: **PETER DE SÈVE**

Art Director: VALERIE BROCHARD

Agency: KLEMTNER ADVERTISING

Client: KLEMTNER ADVERTISING

315

Artist: **GREG HARGREAVES**

Art Director: BRENT BOYD

Agency: C.M.F. AND 2

Client: IOWA LOTTERY

316

Artist: **PATTY DRYDEN**

Agency: VIGON & SEIREENI

Client: HARARI

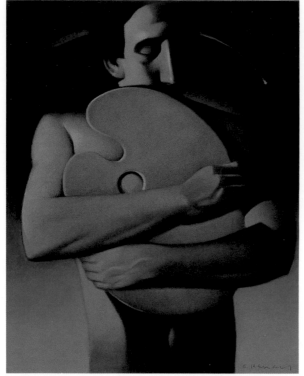

313

314

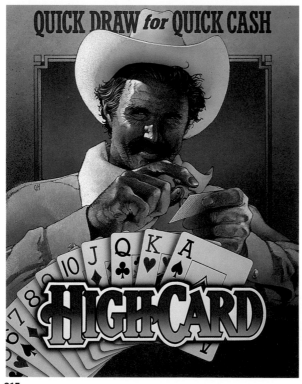

315

316

317

Artist: **PAUL DAVIS**

Art Director: PAUL DAVIS

Client: NEW YORK SHAKESPEARE
FESTIVAL

ILLUSTRATORS31

318

Artist: **JOHN H. HOWARD**

Art Director: STEVEN BYRAM

Client: CBS RECORDS

319

Artist: **EDWARD ABRAMS**

Art Director: MARVIN SCHWARTZ

Client: ANGEL RECORDS

318

319

320

321

ILLUSTRATORS31

322

Artist: **STEVE BRODNER**

Art Director: STEPHEN DOYLE

Client: J&B CAMPAIGN MANUAL

323

Artist: **G. ALLEN GARNS**

Art Director: DEBBIE MEESE

Agency: MULLEN ADVERTISING

Client: NORTHERN ARIZONA TRUST

322

323

324

Artist: **EDWARD ABRAMS**

Art Director: MARVIN SCHWARTZ

Client: ANGEL RECORDS

325

Artist: **GERRY GERSTEN**

Art Director: MICHAEL ROSENBAUM

Agency: OGILVY & MATHER DIRECT

Client: QUALITY PAPERBACK
BOOK CLUB

326

Artist: **G. ALLEN GARNS**

Art Director: DORIS FORTINO

Agency: FORTINO MORIARITY

Client: ST. PAUL CENTER

324

325

326

327

Artist: **LUIS VELEZ**

328

Artist: **PETER KUPER**

Art Director: STACY DRUMMOND

Client: COLUMBIA RECORDS

329

Artist: **PAUL DAVIS**

Art Director: PAUL DAVIS

Client: NEW YORK SHAKESPEARE
FESTIVAL

327

328

329

330

Artist: **RAFAL OLBINSKI**

Art Director: JIM RUSSEK

Agency: RUSSEK ADVERTISING

Client: ORCHESTRA OF ST. LUKES

331

Artist: **STEPHEN BYRAM**

Art Director: TOM ARGAUER

Client: JMT RECORDS

332

Artist: **STEPHEN BYRAM**

Art Director: STEPHEN BYRAM

Client: CBS RECORDS

333

Artist: **JOHN KLEBER**

Art Director: MIKE MAZZA

Client: WILLIAMSON PRINTING

331

332

333

334

Artist: **STEPHEN T. JOHNSON**

Art Director: DEBBIE ROBINSON
ANN WILLOUGHBY

Agency: WILLOUGHBY &
ASSOCIATES

Client: ASSOCIATION OF KANSAS
THEATRE

334

335

Artist: **ROBERT M. CUNNINGHAM**

Art Director: TADASHI MATSUYAMA

Agency: DENTSU, INC.

Client: PANASONIC (MATSUSHITA
ELECTRIC)

336

Artist: **BART FORBES**

Art Director: CLYDE STEELE

Agency: LEO BURNETT ADVERTISING

Client: PHILIP MORRIS

337

Artist: **BOB CROFUT**

Art Director: JIM McCREADY

Client: DRIFTWAY COLLECTION

335

336

337

338

339

340

338

Artist: **GLENN HARRINGTON**

Art Director: KEJI OBATA

Agency: HOASHI STUDIO

Client: TRADD

339

Artist: **GARY OVERACRE**

Art Director: RICHARD MANTEL

Client: NEW YORK

340

Artist: **C. MICHAEL DUDASH**

Art Director: CLYDE STEELE

Agency: LEO BURDETTE ADVERTISING

Client: MARLBORO

341

Artist: **DANIEL PELAVIN**

342

Artist: **DANIEL PELAVIN**

343

Artist: **DOUGLAS FRASER**

Art Director: PAUL ASAO

Agency: CARMICHAEL LYNCH

Client: ALLEN BRADLEY

341

342

343

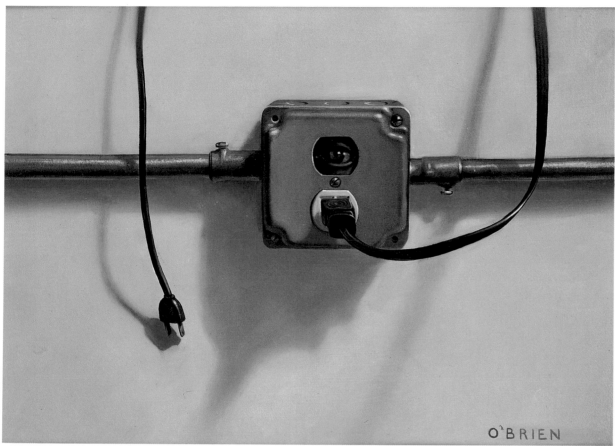

344

Artist: **TIM O'BRIEN**

345

Artist: **CHRIS SPOLLEN**

Art Director: PAT BRYNS

Client: SAN DIEGO GAS AND
ELECTRIC CO.

346

Artist: **CHRIS SPOLLEN**

345

346

347

Artist: **MYLES PINKNEY**

Art Director: NANCY LEWIS

Client: MacGUIDE MAGAZINE

347

348

349

348

Artist: **DAVID LESH**

Art Director: GARY GIBSON

Client: LOTUS DEVELOPMENT

349

Artist: **SANDRA HENDLER**

Art Director: SUEANNE SANNELLA

Client: COMMUNICATIONS WEEK

350

Artist: **JAMES TUGHAN**

Art Director: HOLLY OLDFIELD

Agency: OLDFIELD DAVIS, INC.

Client: METHODIST HOSPITAL
OF DALLAS

350

351

Artist: **KAM MAK**

Art Director: LOUISE KOLLENBAUM

Client: BANANA REPUBLIC

352

Artist: **KRISTEN FUNKHOUSER**

Art Director: PAT BYRNES

Agency: FRANKLIN & ASSOCIATES

Client: SAN DIEGO GAS & ELECTRIC

353

Artist: **JAN MCCOMAS**

Art Director: STACY DRUMMOND

Client: COLUMBIA RECORDS

351

352

353

354

355

354

Artist: **C. MICHAEL DUDASH**

Art Director: BOB TANAKA

Agency: COLE & WEBER

Client: BOEING AIRLINES

355

Artist: **KYOUNGJA LEE**

Art Director: FRANCIS LIVINGSTON

356

Artist: **WILSON McLEAN**

Art Director: GLENN BATKIN

Agency: GREY ADVERTISING

Client: CANON PRINTERS

356

357

358

359

357

Artist: **RAFAL OLBINSKI**

Art Director: NANCY DRAUGHN

Client: HUMANA HOSPITAL—
DALLAS

358

Artist: **RAFAL OLBINSKI**

Art Director: WILLIAM PIERCE

Client: BOWNE & CO.

359

Artist: **ALAN E. COBER**

Art Director: ANNETTE OSTERLUND

Agency: SCALI McCABE

Client: CHASE MANHATTAN BANK

ILLUSTRATORS31

360

Artist: **BILL MAYER**

Art Director: BILL MAYER

Client: THE RIPPINGTONS

361

Artist: **ELWOOD H. SMITH**

Art Director: LESLIE SISMAN
            CAROLINE WALOWSKI

Agency: KALLIR, PHILIPS, ROSS, INC.

Client: GLAXO, INC.

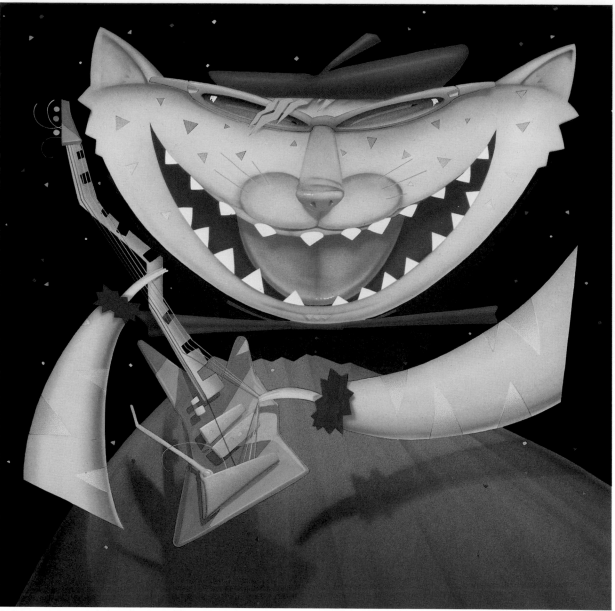

360

361

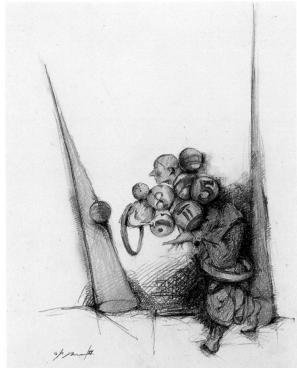

362

363

364

365

362

Artist: **GEOFFREY MOSS**

Art Director: CAROL GOLDEN
PAUL PRUNEAU

Client: APPLE COMPUTERS

363

Artist: **LONNI SUE JOHNSON**

Art Director: ROB THACKER

Agency: ROB THACKER ASSOCIATES

Client: LANDAU'S

364

Artist: **MARK A. FREDRICKSON**

Art Director: DAVID BARTELS

Agency: BARTELS & CARSTENS

Client: DAVID BARTELS

365

Artist: **LINDA HELTON**

Art Director: RON SULLIVAN

Agency: SULLIVAN PERKINS

Client: CITYFAIR

366

Artist: **TERESA FASOLINO**

Art Director: FRAN DAVIES

Agency: MEDICUS

Client: PROCTER & GAMBLE

367

Artist: **CHARLES SANTORE**

Art Director: DON BENDER

Client: JELLYBEAN PRESS

366

367

368

369

370

368

Artist: **BRALDT BRALDS**

Art Director: CURT CHUVALAS

Agency: BLOOMHORST STORY
O'HARA

Client: FIRST MERCHANTS BANK

369

Artist: **CAROL WALD**

Art Director: LENA TABORI

Client: RSVP DIRECTORY

370

Artist: **CHRIS CALLE**

Art Director: CHRIS CALLE

Client: UNICOVER CORPORATION

371

Artist: **BRALDT BRALDS**

Art Director: DAVID BARTELS

Agency: BARTELS & CARSTENS

Client: BUDWEISER

372

Artist: **BRALDT BRALDS**

Art Director: DAVID BARTELS

Agency: BARTELS & CARSTENS

Client: BUDWEISER

371

372

373

Artist: **ROBERT GIUSTI**

Art Director: BOB MANLEY

Agency: ALTMAN & MANLEY

Client: FRENCH TRANSIT LTD.

373

374

Artist: **STEVE MICHAEL SULLIVAN**

Art Director: DIANA HRISINKO

Client: SCHOLASTIC

374

375

Artist: **ROBERT HUNT**

Art Director: SUSANNE EDMONSON

Agency: EISAMAN JOHNS AND LAWS

Client: PENDELTON WOOLEN MILLS

376

Artist: **JACK UNRUH**

Art Director: WOODY LOWE

Agency: HAL RINEY AND PARTNERS

Client: ANHEUSER-BUSCH

377

Artist: **MARK CHICKINELLI**

Client: RIVER CITY ROUNDUP

375

376

377

378

Artist: **ROBERT CRAWFORD**

Art Director: PETER HARRISON
                HAROLD BURCH

Client: BRITISH PETROLEUM

378

379

Artist: **BRENT WATKINSON**

Art Director: JIM DEVIN

Agency: BRYANT LAHEY & BARNES

Client: A.H. SCHERING ANIMAL
HEALTH

380

Artist: **PAUL MICICH**

Art Director: MARY HAMILTON

Client: RCA RECORDS

381

Artist: **WENDELL MINOR**

379

380

381

ILLUSTRATORS31

382

Artist: **BOB CROFUT**

Art Director: WILLIAM HIXSON

Agency: IOLA ASSOCIATES

Client: HOECHST

382

383

Artist: **MURRAY TINKELMAN**

384

Artist: **MURRAY TINKELMAN**

385

Artist: **DAVID GROVE**

Art Director: SUZANNE ELWARD

Agency: DUGAN FARLEY
COMMUNICATIONS

Client: BOEHRINGER INGELHEIM

383

385

384

386

Artist: **DANIEL CRAIG**

Art Director: RUSS AUGER

Agency: J. MacLACHLAN
      & ASSOCIATES

Client: ZYCAD CORPORATION

386

387

Artist: **KIM BEHM**

Art Director: JAY EDELNANT

Client: THEATRE UNI

388

Artist: **JOYCE KITCHELL**

Art Director: FRANCENE
CHRISTIANSON

Agency: SCOTT GRIFFITHS
ADVERTISING

Client: KERR

389

Artist: **JOYCE KITCHELL**

Art Director: FRANCENE
CHRISTIANSON

Agency: SCOTT GRIFFITHS
ADVERTISING

Client: KERR

387

388

389

JURY

GARY KELLEY
GOLD MEDAL

RAFAL OLBINSKI
SILVER MEDAL

**CHUCK McVICKER,
Chairman**
Illustrator

SOREN NORING
Art Director, *Reader's Digest*

ROBERT CRAWFORD
Illustrator

ALAN PECKOLICK
Graphic Designer

PETER FIORE
Illustrator

JILL KARLA SCHWARZ
Illustrator

MELISSA JACOBY
Art Director, Viking Penguin

MICHAEL J. SMOLLIN
Illustrator

ARNIE LEVIN
Illustrator

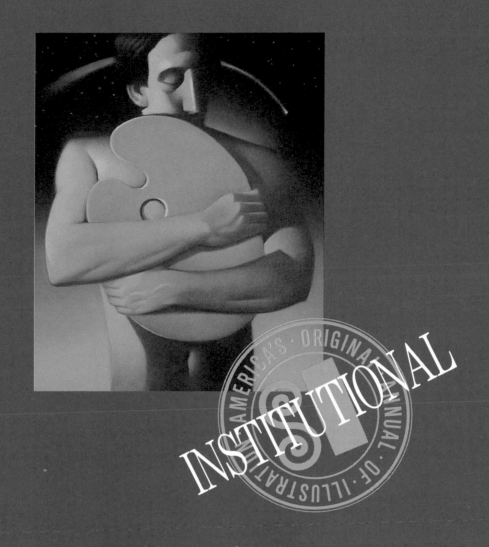

GARY KELLEY

After studying at the University of Northern Iowa, Kelley started his career as a graphic designer, then corporate art director. Eventually he shifted emphasis from design to illustration in the mid-1970s, and now freelances in Cedar Falls, Iowa.

His clients include dozens of major publications, record companies and advertising agencies.

Kelley has received numerous awards from the Society of Illustrators, *American Illustration*, *CA*, and *Print*.

Art Director: SANDRA DI PASQUA

Client: ART DIRECTORS CLUB OF TULSA

RAFAL OLBINSKI

Polish-born Olbinski graduated from Warsaw Polytechnical Institute with a degree in architecture. He found, however, that illustration more fully satisfied his creative needs and in 1968 began designing award-winning posters.

In 1981, while Olbinski was in the United States for an exhibition of his posters, martial law was imposed in Poland. Olbinski decided to remain in New York, where he now works and also teaches at the School of Visual Arts.

Client: AMERICAN FOUNDATION FOR AIDS RESEARCH

392

Artist: **TED CoCONIS**

Art Director: BOB JOHNSON

Agency: JOHNSON & JOYCE

Client: JOHNSON & JOYCE

393

Artist: **CRAIG NELSON**

Art Director: CRAIG NELSON

Client: SOCIETY OF ILLUSTRATORS
OF LOS ANGELES

394

Artist: **WARREN LINN**

Art Director: STEPHEN BYRAM

Client: CBS RECORDS

395

Artist: **PAUL DAVIS**

Art Director: DICK LOOMIS

Agency: THE PAIGE GROUP

Client: MOHAWK PAPER

392

393

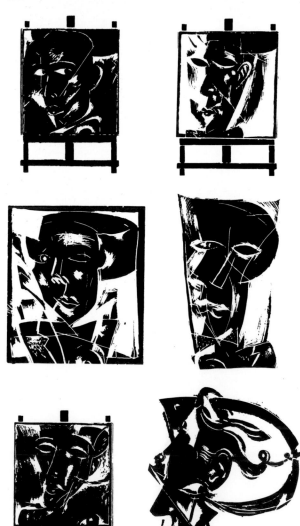

394

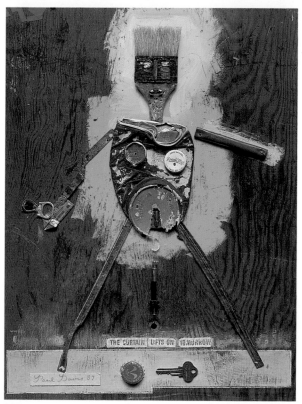

395

396

Artist: **JON ELLIS**

Art Director: JON ELLIS

Client: THE HEART ASSOCIATION
OF AMERICA

397

Artist: **CYNTHIA TORP**

398

Artist: **RONALD H. WENNEKES**

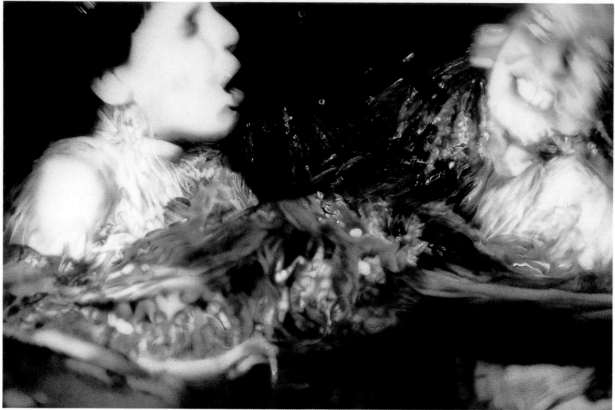

397

398

399

400

401

399

Artist: **DANIEL SCHWARTZ**

400

Artist: **TERRY WIDENER**

Art Director: STEVEN HOFFMAN

Client: NEW YORK UNIVERSITY
MAGAZINE

401

Artist: **JAMES McMULLAN**

Art Director: JAMES McMULLAN

Client: THE HAMPTON LIBRARY
COMMITTEE

ILLUSTRATORS**31**

402

Artist: **JOHN RUSH**

Client: PEMA BROWNE, LTD.

402

403

404

405

Artist: **JOSEF RUBINSTEIN**

Art Director: BURT SILVERMAN

Artist: **JOSEF RUBINSTEIN**

Art Director: BURT SILVERMAN

Artist: **JOSEF RUBINSTEIN**

Art Director: BURT SILVERMAN

404

405

ILLUSTRATORS31

406

Artist: **BRAD HOLLAND**

Art Director: REX PETEET

Client: JAMES RIVER PAPER CO.

407

Artist: **PAUL SCHULENBURG**

Art Director: DOUG EYMER

Client: COMPUTER INTELLIGENCE

408

Artist: **BOB PETERS**

Client: GERALD AND CULLEN
RAPP, INC.

406

407

408

409

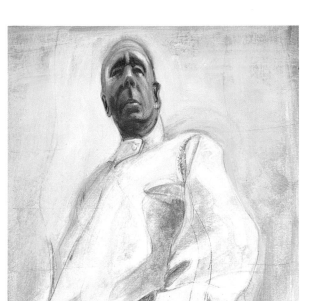

410

409

Artist: **TED WRIGHT**

Art Director: DAN KING

Agency: MARITZ MOTIVATION, INC.

Client: EDS

410

Artist: **KIRK BOTERO**

411

Artist: **BOB PETERS**

Client: GERALD AND CULLEN
RAPP, INC.

412

Artist: **GEORGE Y. ABE**

Art Director: JAMI MIYAMOTO

Agency: ADVERTISING DESIGNERS

Client: CITY NATIONAL
CORPORATION

411

412

413

Artist: **TOM CURRY**

Art Director: SUSAN CURRY
TOM CURRY

Client: ADVANCED GRAPHICS
SYSTEMS

413

414

415

414

Artist: **KEN KRUG**

415

Artist: **LONNI SUE JOHNSON**

Art Director: TOM HUGHES
MARK KELLY

Client: LOTUS DEVELOPMENT CORP.

ILLUSTRATORS31

416

Artist: **RON BECKHAM**

Art Director: LARRY HANES

Client: CINCOM SYSTEMS

417

Artist: **SCOTT REYNOLDS**

Art Director: JEFFERY LEDER

418

Artist: **ROBERT RODRIGUEZ**

Art Director: ROBERT FITCH

Client: PAPER MOON GRAPHICS

416

417

418

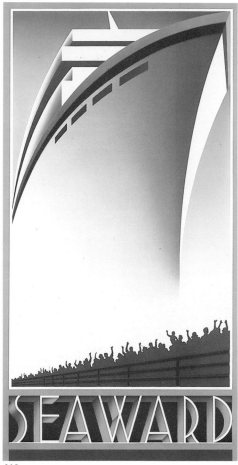

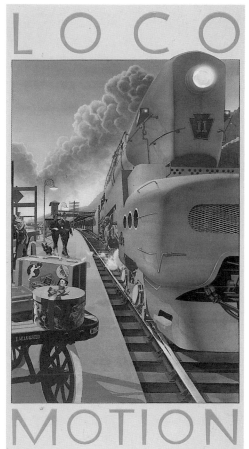

419

Artist: **NICK GAETANO**

Art Director: VAN EARLY

Agency: McKINNEY & SILVER

Client: NORWEGIAN CRUISE LINE

420

Artist: **JOHN P. MAGGARD III**

Art Director: JOHN P. MAGGARD III
JOE STRYKER

Client: AMERICAN HEART
ASSOCIATION

421

Artist: **CARY HENRIE**

Art Director: KATHLEEN HOWELL

Client: MANHARDT-ALEXANDER

419

420

421

ILLUSTRATORS31

422

Artist: **YUTAKA SASAKI**

Art Director: RAYNE BEAUDOIN

Agency: TYCER FULTZ BELLACK

Client: SEATTLE AQUARIUM

423

Artist: **PETER SIS**

Art Director: JANETTE BROD

Client: CHILDREN'S BOOK COUNCIL

424

Artist: **GUY BILLOUT**

Art Director: CHARLES KRELOFF

Client: WORKMAN PUBLISHING

425

Artist: **ALAN E. COBER**

Art Director: DON SHANOSKY

Client: SQUIBB

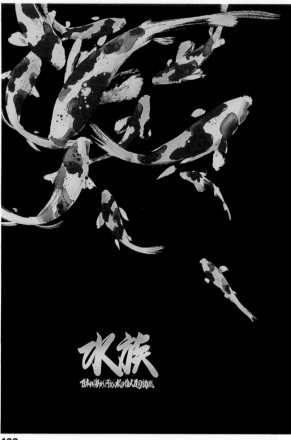

422

423

424

425

426

Artist: **RAFAL OLBINSKI**

Art Director: RAFAL OLBINSKI

Client: DEL BELLO GALLERY

427

Artist: **FRANCIS LIVINGSTON**

Art Director: SHELLY WEIR

Agency: KOLMAN SUITOR
ADVERTISING

Client: DiMARE

428

Artist: **SANDRA SPEIDEL**

429

Artist: **JANE STERRETT**

427

428

429

430

Artist: **JOHN H. HOWARD**

Art Director: MICHAEL ROCK

Client: SHEARSON LEHMAN
HUTTON

431

Artist: **MICHELE MANNING**

432

Artist: **JACK MOLLOY**

Art Director: SHEILA BERIGAN

Client: NICOLLET ISLAND INN

431

430

433

Artist: **VICTOR LAZZARO**

Art Director: JOHN MITCHELL

Client: TOWN OF REDDING,
CONNECTICUT

434

Artist: **RICHARD SPARKS**

432

433

434

435

Artist: **BRYAN HAYNES**

Art Director: DIANA DAWES

Agency: MECHANICAL LADY

435

436

437

438

439

436

Artist: **RICHARD THOMPSON**

437

Artist: **JOHN A. MONTELEONE**

438

Artist: **DAVID LESH**

Art Director: MILES HUTCHENS

Client: ADDISON CONSULTANCY
GROUP

439

Artist: **MARK ENGLISH**

Art Director: MIKE SCRICCO

Agency: KEILER ADVERTISING

Client: STRATHMORE PAPER

ILLUSTRATORS31

440

Artist: **JOHN JUDE PALENCAR**

Art Director: JOHN JUDE PALENCAR

Client: BYRON PREISS VISUAL
PUBLICATIONS

441

Artist: **LAURA MEADOWS**

442

Artist: **KIM BEHM**

Art Director: TONY LUETKEHANS

Client: GUTHRIE THEATRE

443

Artist: **TIM JESSELL**

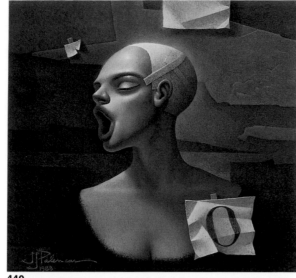

440

441

442

443

444

Artist: **GARY KELLEY**

Art Director: TONY RUTKA

Client: DREW UNIVERSITY

ILLUSTRATORS31

445

Artist: **BOB CONGE**

Art Director: BOB CONGE

Client: COMMUNICATOR OF THE
YEAR AWARDS

446

Artist: **MURRAY TINKELMAN**

Art Director: MO LEBOWITZ

Client: U&lc.

447

Artist: **RANDALL ENOS**

448

Artist: **BURT SILVERMAN**

Art Director: JERRY HERRING

Client: SIMPSON PAPER CO.

445

446

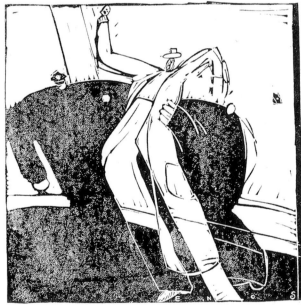

447

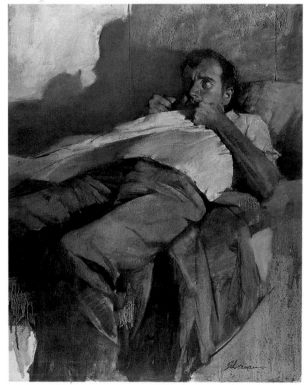

448

449

450

449

Artist: **JOHN RAMHORST**

Art Director: MARVIN MATTELSON

Client: SCHOOL OF VISUAL ARTS

450

Artist: **GEORGE FERNANDEZ**

451

Artist: **CLIFFORD FAUST**

451

ILLUSTRATORS31

452

Artist: **GARY RUDDELL**

Art Director: GARY RUDDELL

Client: BAEN BOOKS

452

453

454

455

453

Artist: **ANITA KUNZ**

Art Director: ANITA KUNZ
PAT SLOAN

Client: DALLAS SOCIETY
OF ILLUSTRATORS

454

Artist: **EDWARD S. GAZSI**

455

Artist: **ROBERT GOLDSTROM**

Art Director: EDWIN TORRES

Client: SCHOLASTIC

ILLUSTRATORS31

456

Artist: **BILL BRUNING**

Art Director: BOB BARRIE

Agency: FALLON McELLIGOTT

Client: FEDERAL EXPRESS

456

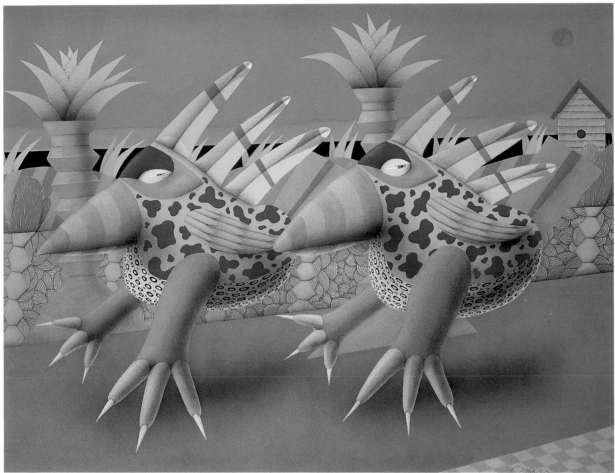

457

457

Artist: **T.P. SPEER**

Art Director: T.P. SPEER

Client: CAMERON PUBLISHING

458

Artist: **GREGORY HALLY**

459

Artist: **T.E. BREITENBACH**

Client: MEANMAN MARKETING

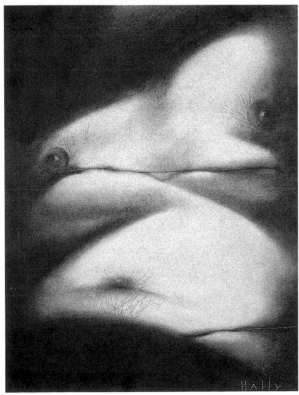

458

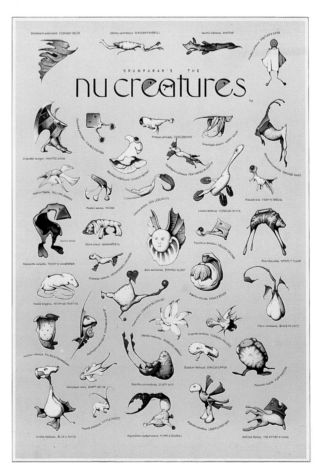

459

460

Artist: **TIM JESSELL**

460

461

461

Artist: **CRAIG McFARLAND BROWN**

Client: ROCKRIMMON PRESS

462

Artist: **BRYAN HAYNES**

Art Director: BRYAN HAYNES

Client: ELDRIDGE & ASSOCIATES

463

Artist: **BOB PETERS**

Client: GERALD AND CULLEN RAPP, INC.

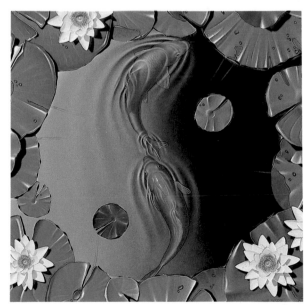

463

462

464

Artist: **DOUGLAS ANDELIN**

Art Director: EDWIN TORRES

Client: SCHOLASTIC

465

Artist: **LORI LOHSTOETER**

Art Director: PAUL ELLIOTT

466

Artist: **PATRICIA DOKTOR**

Art Director: JOEL NAKAMURA

464

465

466

467

Artist: **JUNE M. BROCK**

Client: HALLMARK CARDS

468

Artist: **JAMES McMULLAN**

Art Director: MICHAEL GERICKE

Client: DREXEL BURNHAM
LAMBERT

469

Artist: **NEIL ORLOWSKI
JED PORTER**

Client: HALLMARK CARDS

467

468

469

470

Artist: **LISA FRENCH**

Art Director: HAROLD BURCH
PETER HARRISON

Client: BRITISH PETROLEUM

471

Artist: **MICHAEL DAVID BROWN**

Art Director: MICHAEL DAVID BROWN

Client: FRANKLIN SQUARE
HOSPITAL CENTER

472

Artist: **EUGENE HOFFMAN**

Art Director: ALEGRA ALEINIKOFF

Client: LONGMONT FOODS

470

471

472

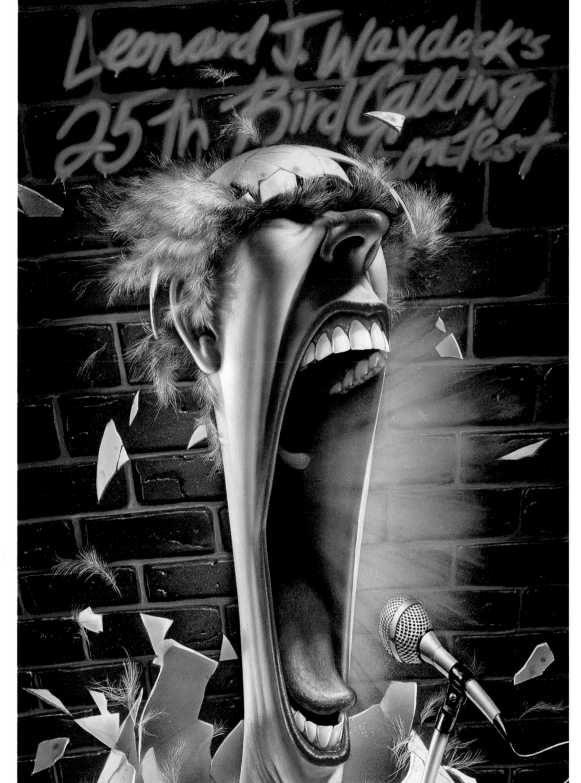

473

Artist: **MARK A. FREDRICKSON**

Art Director: DAVID BARTELS

Agency: BARTELS & CARSTENS

Client: PIEDMONT HIGH SCHOOL

474

Artist: **DELRO ROSCO**

475

Artist: **BARRY FITZGERALD**

Art Director: ALAN E. COBER
KATHLEEN C. HOWELL

Client: MANHARDT-ALEXANDER

474

475

476

477

478

476

Artist: **CRAIG FRAZIER**

Art Director: CRAIG FRAZIER

Client: FRIDAY NIGHT LIVE

477

Artist: **FRANCIS LIVINGSTON**

Client: FREDA SCOTT

478

Artist: **BOB DORSEY**

Art Director: ROBERT MARKS
　　　　　　　BOB DORSEY

Client: NEWTON FALLS PAPER MILL

479

Artist: **THOMAS BUCHS**

Art Director: THOMAS BUCHS

Client: THE ART FACTORY

479

480

481

482

480

Artist: **JIM LAMBRENOS**

Art Director: JIM LAMBRENOS

Client: PHOTOTYPE COLOR
GRAPHICS

481

Artist: **DAVE LA FLEUR**

Art Director: STAN WEIR

Agency: QUILLEN ELSEA JANZEN

Client: WICHITA CHAPTER
OF A.I.G.A.

482

Artist: **KAZUHIKO SANO**

489

Artist: **DOUGLAS FRASER**

Art Director: ART WORTHINGTON
TOM FOWLER

Client: OAKLAND A'S

490

Artist: **FRANK A. STEINER**

Art Director: MIKE TURNER

Client: MARITZ MOTIVATION CO.

491

Artist: **KAZUHIKO SANO**

Art Director: STEVE WATSON

Client: VISA INTERNATIONAL

489

490

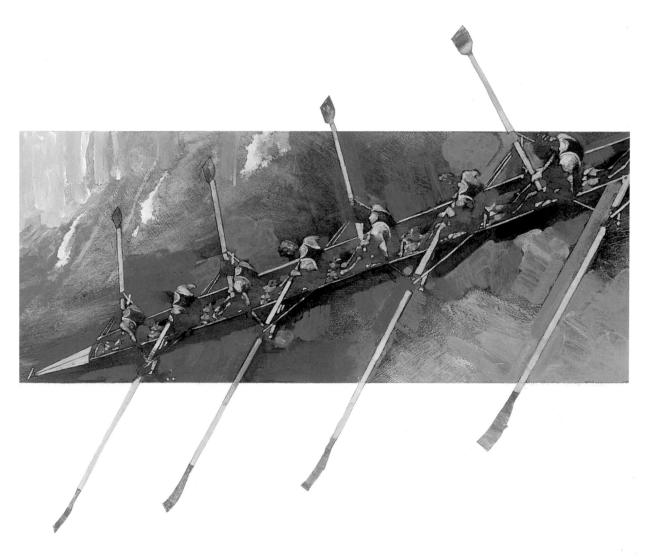

491

492

492

Artist: **HOWARD SCHWARTZBERG**

493

Artist: **C.F. PAYNE**

Art Director: RICHARD SOLOMON

494

Artist: **FRANCIS LIVINGSTON**

Art Director: MARCEL SCHURMAN

Client: MARCEL SCHURMAN CO.

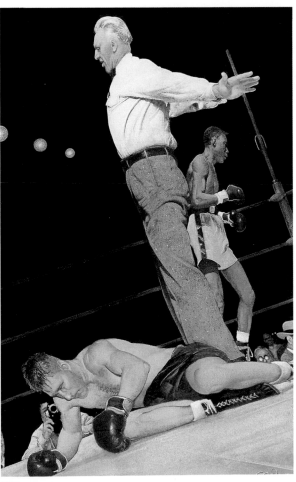

493

494

495

Artist: **PETER SIS**

Art Director: MITSUTOSHI HOSAKA

Client: MATSUZAKI SHOJI

496

Artist: **JACK UNRUH**

Art Director: MITSUTOSHI HOSAKA

Client: DAI NIPPON PRINTING

497

Artist: **JOHN CEBALLOS**

Art Director: TONY LUETKEHANS

Client: GUTHRIE THEATRE

495

496

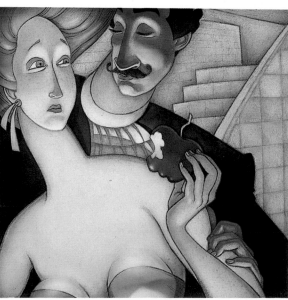

497

498

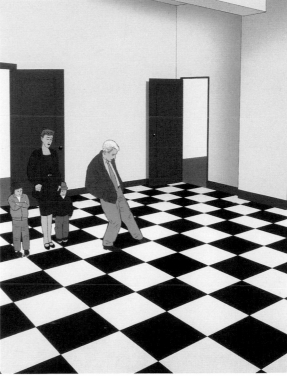

499

498

Artist: **KEN THOMPSON**

499

Artist: **GUY BILLOUT**

Art Director: CHARLES KRELOFF

Client: WORKMAN PUBLISHING

500

Artist: **JACK UNRUH**

Art Director: JERRY HERRING

Client: SIMPSON PAPER CO.

501

Artist: **BURT SILVERMAN**

Art Director: JEFF RICH

Client: THE BAXTER FOUNDATION

500

501

ILLUSTRATORS31

502

Artist: **JOHN THOMPSON**

Client: U.S. AIR FORCE

503

Artist: **GERRY GERSTEN**

Art Director: MARILYN HOFFNER

Client: COOPER UNION

504

Artist: **ADAM NIKLEWICZ**

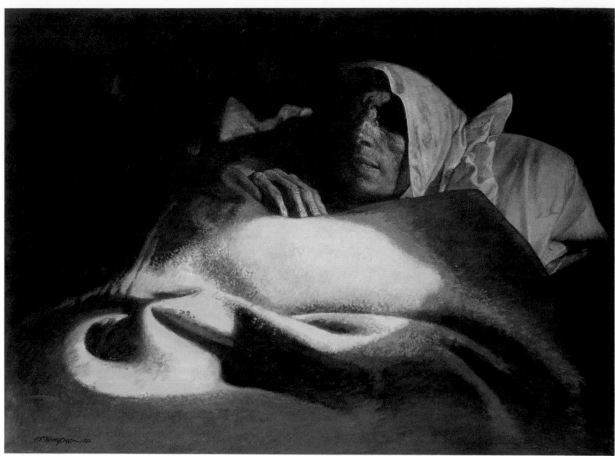

502

503

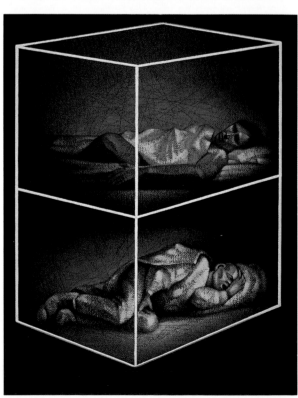

504

505

Artist: **BART FORBES**

Art Director: JOE GULSTINE

Client: WESTOVER EDITIONS

506

Artist: **JAMES ENNIS KIRKLAND**

Art Director: ALFREDO MUCCINO

Agency: MUCCINO DESIGN

Client: W.A. KRUEGER CO.

505

506

ILLUSTRATORS31

507

Artist: **ROBERT HEINDEL**

Art Director: ANNA LEWIS

Client: THE OBSESSION OF
DANCE CO.

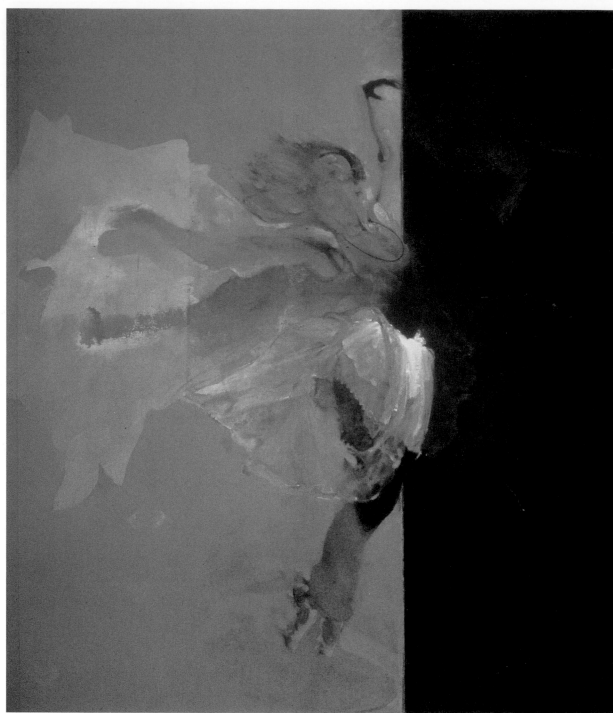

507

508

509

508

Artist: **ROBERT HEINDEL**

Art Director: ANNA LEWIS

Client: THE OBSESSION
OF DANCE CO.

509

Artist: **CAROL WALD**

510

Artist: **GARY KELLEY**

Art Director: JOHN HALL

Client: HOPKINS CENTER/
DARTMOUTH COLLEGE

511

Artist: **JACK UNRUH**

Art Director: BOB DOWNS

Client: HERITAGE PRESS

510

511

ILLUSTRATORS 31

512

Artist: **RANDALL ENOS**

513

Artist: **ELIZABETH WOLF**

Art Director: ROBERT SUGAR

Client: WORLD MUSIC PRODUCTIONS

514

Artist: **BOB CONGE**

Art Director: BOB CONGE

Client: VIETNAM VETERANS
OF AMERICA

515

Artist: **JOHN KASCHT**

512

513

514

515

516

Artist: **JOHN H. HOWARD**

Art Director: ART JONES

Agency: BRANNIGAN-DeMARCO

Client: CALTRATE

516

517

Artist: **ROBERT HEINDEL**

Art Director: ANNA LEWIS

Client: THE OBSESSION
OF DANCE CO.

518

Artist: **DOUG JOHNSON**

Art Director: DOUG JOHNSON

Client: NEW YORK STATE
URBAN DEVELOPMENT
CORPORATION

519

Artist: **GERRY GERSTEN**

Art Director: MARILYN HOFFNER

Client: COOPER UNION

517

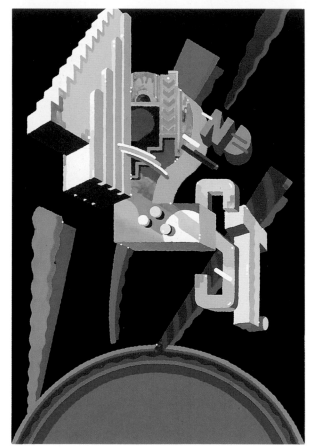

518

519

520

521

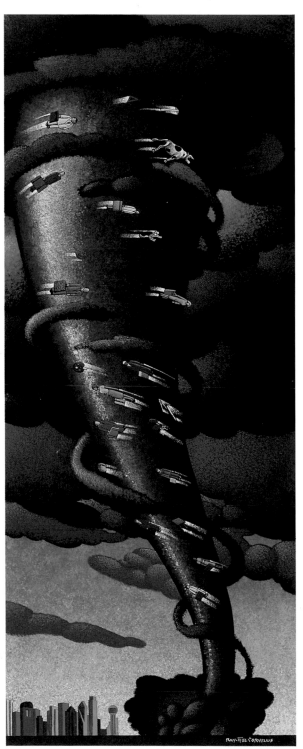

522

520

Artist: **MILTON GLASER**

Art Director: JESSICA WEBER

Client: THE JUILLIARD SCHOOL

521

Artist: **JAMES McMULLAN**

Art Director: BILL FREELAND

Client: PARK WEST HIGH SCHOOL

522

Artist: **RAY-MEL CORNELIUS**

Art Director: DON CRUM

Client: INTERNATIONAL
ASSOCIATION OF BUSINESS
COMMUNICATORS

ILLUSTRATORS31

523

Artist: **ARDEN VON HAEGER**

Art Director: CARL HERMANN

Client: THE HON COMPANY

524

Artist: **RICHARD SPARKS**

Art Director: JOHN J. CONLEY

Client: EXXON

525

Artist: **BERNIE FUCHS**

Art Director: BERNIE FUCHS

Client: MASER PUBLISHING

526

Artist: **SALLY WERN COMPORT**

Client: W/C STUDIO

523

524

525

526

527

527

Artist: **BRAD HOLLAND**

Art Director: WOODY PIRTLE

Client: NCR CORPORATION

528

Artist: **CAMA CHALL-SZALEWICZ**

528

ILLUSTRATORS 31

529

Artist: **PETER M. FIORE**

Art Director: JERRY ALTEN

Client: TV GUIDE

530

Artist: **BART FORBES**

Art Director: JERRY HERRING

Client: SIMPSON PAPER CO.

531

Artist: **DON WELLER**

Art Director: DON WELLER

Client: DALLAS SOCIETY OF
       VISUAL COMMUNICATION

529

530

531

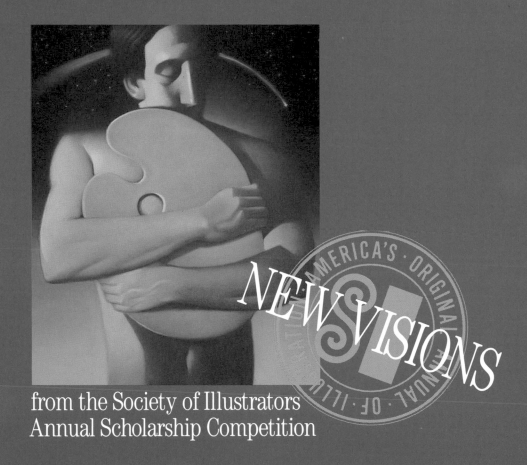

NEW VISIONS

from the Society of Illustrators
Annual Scholarship Competition

NEW VISIONS

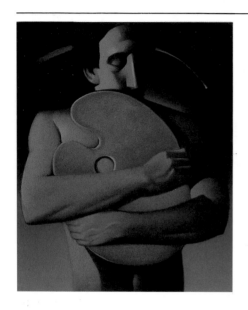

The future lies with the young. This is true in illustration and the young artists emerging from their years of training are the pool from which the most talented and determined will emerge and succeed. So, for the first time, we have included the work selected for the Society of Illustrators Annual Scholarship Competition because we want you to have the first look at the future.

Over four thousand entries poured in from the many excellent and highly directed, college-level art and design schools across the country. Chairman, Eileen Hedy Schultz and Co-Chairman Peter Fiore guided the judges through the lengthy process of selection and from those entries the following 116 were chosen for their technique, insight, and artistry. All pieces were shown at the Society of Illustrators Museum of American Illustration at their Annual Scholarship Exhibition.

In addition to the technical skills being taught in today's art schools, the young people are also getting training in the business of illustration and, as shown in the work prepared for this exhibition, they are getting a taste of competition. And competition is what each and every illustrator working today must face.

It is likely that many of the names you see here will soon be judged by the Society's Annual juries as these students become professionals who have fulfilled their early promise.

The Society of Illustrators

ANNUAL SCHOLARSHIP COMPETITION 1989

PRESIDENT'S MESSAGE

It is possible to become proficient in illustration on one's own, but school hastens discovery and stimulates our imagination. We learn to solve problems, translate the word into graphic images, develop skill with media and techniques and become familiar with basic rules of good design and composition.

These things become part of our unconscious intuitive selves that "feel" when something is right. It also gives us the understanding of why, sometimes, breaking the rules can be a stroke of genius.

Illustration is for the dedicated, inspired and tenacious. There is no guarantee of success. Our careers are a constant struggle to learn, perfect and experiment. But for the successful there is the heavy desire to "Give something back to the profession."

We wish to thank the Hallmark Corporate Foundation, which has substantially supported the program for many years along with The Starr Foundation, The Reader's Digest Association, The Estate of Edna Dorne, The Friends of the Institute of Commercial Art, The Kirchoff/Wohlberg Company in memory of Frances Means, Diamandis Communications, Jellybean Photographics, The Norman Rockwell Museum at Stockbridge, and to those who contributed in memory of Walter Hortens, John Moodie, Harry Rosenbaum and Euclid Shook.

We also wish to thank Beverly Sacks for her inspired chairmanship of the Annual Christmas Auction, a major fundraiser for the Scholarship programs, and the members who so generously donate artwork to it.

On behalf of the Society of Illustrators I wish to congratulate all the students in the show. We wish you a long and healthy career and hope, years from now, you too may be in the position to give back to a profession that has been rewarding to you.

DIANE DILLON
President of the Society, 1987–1989

THE AWARDS

RENÉ ADE

Robert Hunt, Instructor
Academy of Art College
$2,500 Society of Illustrators Award

CHUCK EICHTEN

Bunny Carter, Instructor
San Jose State University
$2,000 Jellybean Photographics Award

AARON GOLAND

Deanna Leamon, Instructor
Milwaukee Institute of Art and Design
$2,000 The Starr Foundation Award

CHRIS LUNDY

David Mocarski, Instructor
Art Center, College of Design
$2,000 Robert H. Blattner Award

RENÉ ADE

CHUCK EICHTEN

AARON GOLAND

CHRIS LUNDY

WINSON TRANG

David Grove, Instructor
Academy of Art College
$2,000 Reader's Digest Association, Inc. Award

MARY MacFARLAND

Paul Jasmin, Instructor
Art Center College of Design
$1,500 The Starr Foundation Award

TERRE RITCHIE

Jon MacDonald, Instructor
Kendall College of Art and Design
$1,500 The Starr Foundation Award

DORIS VINTON

Ralph Allured, Instructor
Kendall College of Art and Design
$1,500 Reader's Digest Association, Inc. Award

ANTONIO WADE

Chris Bartlett, Instructor
Maryland College of Art and Design
$1,500 Reader's Digest Association, Inc. Award

WINSON TRANG

TERRE RITCHIE

MARY MacFARLAND

ANTONIO WADE

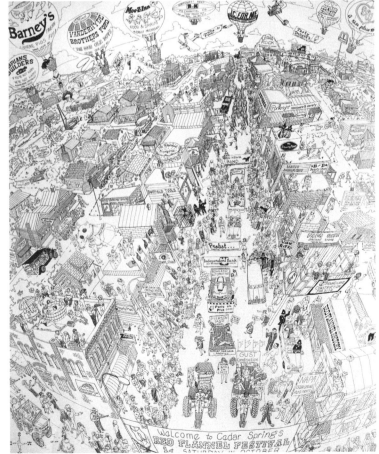

DORIS VINTON

KERRI DERING

Peter Caras, Instructor
duCret School of the Arts
$1,000 Kirchoff/Wohlberg Award
  in Memory of Frances Means

SUSAN GAURIE

Richard Hull, Instructor
Brigham Young University
$1,000 The Norman Rockwell Museum
  at Stockbridge Award

LAURIE KELLER

Jon MacDonald, Instructor
Kendall College of Art and Design
$1,000 Albert Dorne Award

LAURA PHILLIPS

Jim Salvati, Instructor
Art Center College of Design
$1,000 Friends of The Institute of
  Commercial Art Award

JAMES RANSOME

Joseph Rossi, Instructor
Art Students League
$1,000 Jellybean Photographics Award

DAVE REITER

Don Long, Instructor
Colorado Institute of Art
$1,000 The Normal Rockwell Museum
  at Stockbridge Award

KERRI DERING

SUSAN GAURIE

LAURIE KELLER

LAURA PHILLIPS

JAMES RANSOME

DAVE REITER

PERRY STEWART

Glen Edwards, Instructor
Utah State University
$1,000 Diamandis Communications Inc. Award

JOHN THORNTON

Ron Tardino, Instructor
Columbus College of Art and Design
$1,000 Albert Dorne Award

TRAVIS FOSTER

Larry Kresek, Instructor
Ringling School of Art and Design
$750 Award in Memory of Euclid Shook

CRAIG FREEMAN

Bob Ziering, Instructor
Pratt Institute
$750 Award in Memory of John Moodie

FARSHAD LANJANI

Ron Tardino, Instructor
Columbus College of Art and Design
$750 Award in Memory of Harry Rosenbaum

DONALD TERRY JR.

Ashley Hostetter, Instructor
Art Institute of Houston
$750 Award in Memory of Walter Hortens

PERRY STEWART

TRAVIS FOSTER

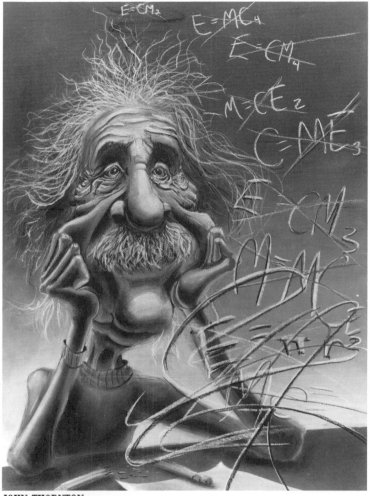

JOHN THORNTON

FARSHAD LANJANI

CRAIG FREEMAN

DONALD TERRY JR.

JILL BARNES

Jon MacDonald, Instructor
Kendall College of Art and Design
$500 Effie Bowie Award

MARK ELLIOTT

Marvin Mattelson, Instructor
School of Visual Arts
$500 Society of Illustrators Award

JEFFREY KELLY

Curt Johnson, Instructor
Kendall College of Art and Design
$500 Adolph Treidler Award

DORI SPECTOR

Harvey Dinnerstein, Instructor
Art Students League
$500 Phillips/Rodewig Award

DORIAN VALLEJO

Brian Bailey, Instructor
School of Visual Arts
$500 Society of Illustrators Award

CHRISTOPHER SHORT

James Santiago, Instructor
Syracuse University
The American Journal of Nursing
    Commission Award

JILL BARNES

MARK ELLIOTT

JEFFREY KELLY

DORIAN VALLEJO

DORI SPECTOR

CHRISTOPHER SHORT

THE EXHIBITION

1

2

3

4

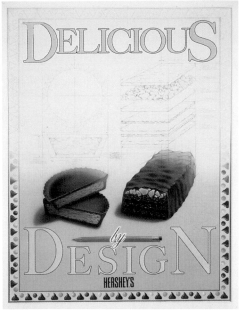

5

6

7

8

9

10

11

12

13

16

14

17

18

15

19

20

21

22

27

23

24

25

29

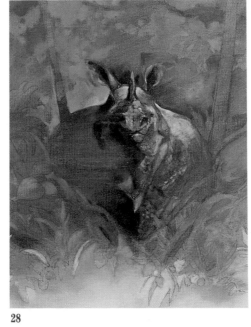

28

26

30 STARR HENDERSON

Curt Johnson, Instructor
Kendall College of Art and Design

31 JOSEPH HICKS

Dennis Nolan, Instructor
Hartford Art School, University of Hartford

32 DARRIN HOOVER

Jerry Kalback, Instructor
Kent State University

33 MARIANNE HUGHES

Deborah Healy, Instructor
Moore College of Art

34 RANCE JONES

Larry Simpson, Instructor
University of North Texas

35 JOLIE JOSEPH

Kathleen O'Connell, Instructor
Herron School of Art

36 PATRICIA KELLEY

Charles Scalin, Instructor
Virginia Commonwealth University

37 JEFFREY KELLY

Jon MacDonald, Instructor
Kendall College of Art and Design

38 ZEEK KROPF

Glen Edwards, Instructor
Utah State University

39 FARSHAD LANJANI

Ron Tardino, Instructor
Columbus College of Art and Design

30

32

31

33

34

35

36

38

37

39

40

41

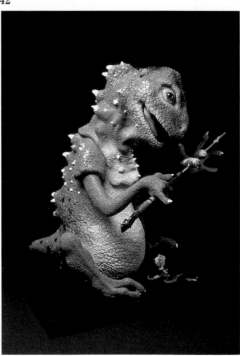

42

43

44

45

46

49

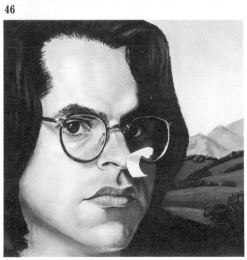

47

48

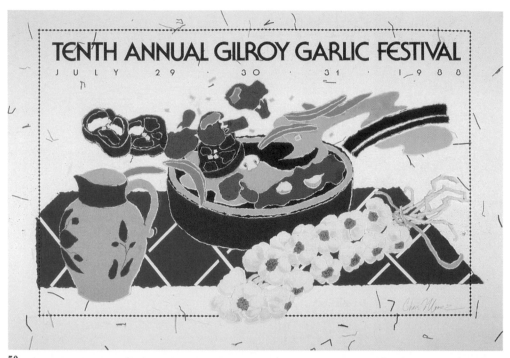

50

52

56

57

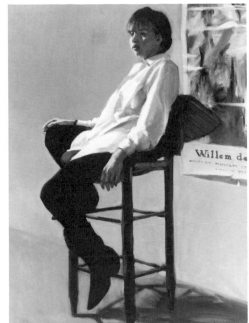

51

53

54

55

58

61

60

62

59

63

65

64

66

67

68 ADAM SCHECHTER

Jack Endewelt, Instructor
School of Visual Arts

69 MICHAEL SCHOLZ

Gerry Lynas, Instructor
Pratt Institute

69A PHILLIP SINGER

Marvin Mattelson, Instructor
School of Visual Arts

70 PERRY STEWART

Glen Edwards, Instructor
Utah State University

71 SHARON SULLIVAN

Cortney Grannek, Instructor
San Jose State University

72 ANTHONY SZCZUDLO

Rich Kryczka, Instructor
American Academy of Art

73 C. MICHAEL TAYLOR

Ron Tardino, Instructor
Columbus College of Art and Design

74 JUDY TAYLOR

Leo Neufeld, Instructor
National Academy of Design

75 MIKE TOFANELLI

Robert Hunt, Instructor
Academy of Art College

76 MIKE TOFANELLI

Robert Hunt, Instructor
Academy of Art College

77 WINSON TRANG

David Grove, Instructor
Academy of Art College

78 MAY TRIEN

Harvey Dinnerstein, Instructor
Art Students League

68

70

69

72

69A

71

73

74

77

75

76

78

80

81

83

79

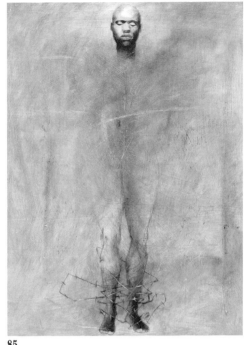

85

86

84

87

88

82

HALLMARK CORPORATE FOUNDATION MATCHING GRANTS

The Hallmark Corporate Foundation of Kansas City, Missouri, is again this year supplying full matching grants for all of the awards in the Society's Student Scholarship Competition. Grants, restricted to the Illustration Departments, are awarded to the following institutions:

$5,000	Kendall College of Art and Design
$4,500	Academy of Art College
$4,500	Art Center College of Design
$2,000	Milwaukee Institute of Art and Design
$2,000	San Jose State University
$1,750	Columbus College of Art and Design
$1,500	Art Students League
$1,500	Maryland College of Art and Design
$1,000	Brigham Young University
$1,000	Colorado Institute of Art
$1,000	duCret School of the Arts
$1,000	School of Visual Arts
$1,000	Utah State University
$750	Art Institute of Houston
$750	Pratt Institute
$750	Ringling School of Art

To contact the artists who appear in this section, please call the Society of Illustrators (212) 838-2560. An updated file on the students, whether still in school or graduated, will be available to interested parties.

ACKNOWLEDGEMENTS

JURORS

Richard Anderson	Sandy Kossin
Victor Closi	Al Lorenz
Gerry Counihan	Dennis Lyall
Kinuko Craft	Richard Mantel
Bill Farnsworth	Rick McCollum
Neil Hardy	Ann Meisel
Mitchell Hooks	Bob Prestopino
Phil Kimmelman	Jeffrey Terreson

ADMINISTRATION

Terrence Brown	Norma Pimsler
Ray Alma	Frederic Taraba
Phyllis Harvey	

ARTIST INDEX

Art Directors, Clients, Agencies

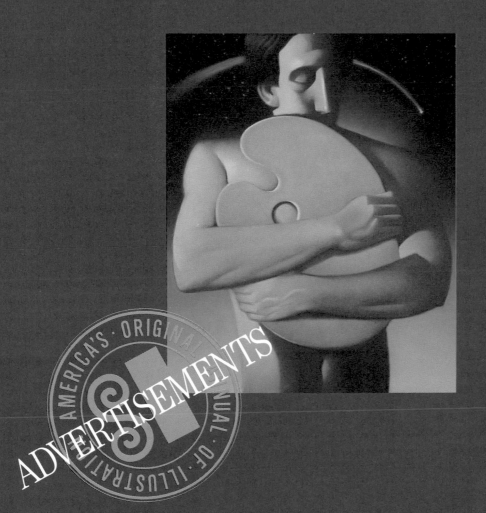

ARTCO

Gail Thurm and Jeff Palmer

Serving New York City clients:
232 Madison Avenue, Suite 600, New York, New York 10016 (212) 889-8777

Serving clients outside New York City:
227 Godfrey Road, Weston, Connecticut 06883 (203) 222-8777

Additional work may be seen in American Showcase Vols. 10, 11, 12 and 13.

Jeff Cornell

Leslie Szabo

Kathy Jeffers

Gary Glover

Lisa Henderling

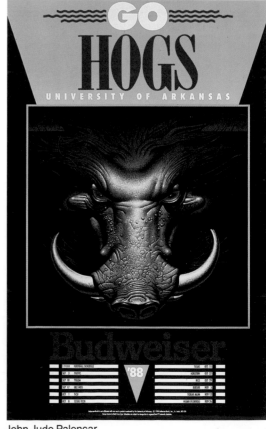

John Jude Palencar

Rick McCollum

Alain Chang

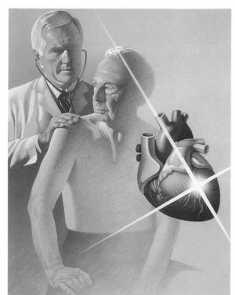

Ed Acuna

Jean Restivo

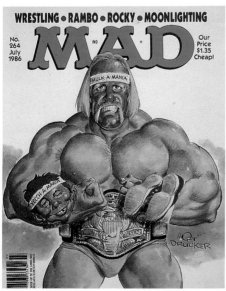

Mort Drucker

Ed Gazsi

ARTCO
Gail Thurm and Jeff Palmer

Serving New York City clients:
232 Madison Avenue, Suite 600, New York, New York 10016 (212) 889-8777

Serving clients outside New York City:
227 Godfrey Road, Weston, Connecticut 06883 (203) 222-8777

Additional work may be seen in American Showcase Vols. 10, 11, 12 and 13.

Edmond Alexander

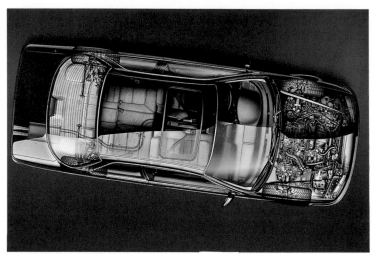

Beau and Alan Daniels

Bob Dacey

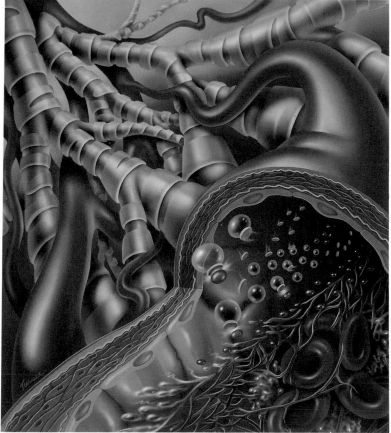

Cynthia Turner

Marcel Rozenberg

Anne Cook

Sally Vitsky

George Angelini

Lisa Falkenstern

Gene Boyer

Dan Brown

Barry Phillips

KIRCHOFF /

866 United Nations Plaza, New York, NY 10017   212-644-2020

897 Boston Post Road, Madison, CT 06443   203-245-7308

WOHLBERG

Illustration copyright © 1989 Lois Ehlert
FROM THUMP, THUMP, Rat-a-Tat-Tat
WRITTEN BY Gene Baer, ILLUSTRATED BY Lois Ehlert
PUBLISHED BY Harper & Row, Publishers

ARTISTS REPRESENTATIVE

DON BRAUTIGAM

NORMAN WALKER

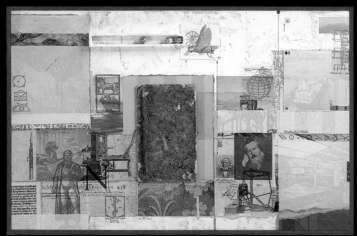

STEVE KARCHIN

ROBERT HEINDEL

MICHAEL DEAS

NORMAN ADAMS

FRED OTNES

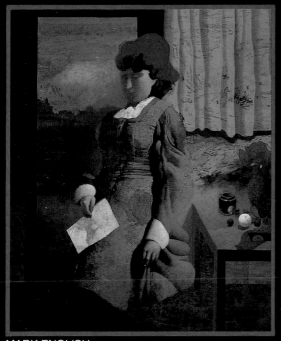

MARK ENGLISH

MICHAEL DUDASH

DICK KREPEL

SKIP LIEPKE

BILL ERLACHER ARTISTS ASSOCIATES

■ 211 EAST 51ST STREET ■ NEW YORK, NEW YORK 10022 ■ TELEPHONE (212)755-1365/6 ■ NICOLE EDELL ASSOCIATE

THE FINE ART
OF STOCK

*From master illustrator **Robert Peak**, recipient of **The Society of Illustrators Hall of Fame** and **Hamilton King Award**, to newer talents who have mastered the art of stock illustration, The Image Bank represents an enviable roster of artists in our international network of 51 offices. Submit portfolios for review to Robert Morris at our Corporate Headquarters, 111 FIFTH AVENUE, NEW YORK CITY 10003, (212) 529-6700.*

STOCK PHOTOGRAPHY
STOCK FILM
STOCK ILLUSTRATION

THE **IMAGE** BANK®

JEFF MANGIAT

CHRIS NOTARILE

JOHN SOLIE

ALFONS
KIEFER

BILL JAMES

DAVID SCHLEINKOFER

GARRY COLBY

JOANN DALEY

PETER M. FIORE

JIM DENEEN

MIKE WIMMER

DAVID HENDERSON

BILL MAUGHAN   JEFFREY LYNCH

Art

These drawings by Frank Hnat are copyrighted by the artist and may not be reproduced for any reason without written permission from the artist.

KOH-I-NOOR
RAPIDOGRAPH®
a **rotring** company

Please send complimentary Catalog No. 3 describing Rapidograph technical pens, drawing inks and other artist materials.

☐ Please send me the names of Koh-I-Noor dealers in my area.

NAME *(Please print or type)*

COMPANY *(If the following is a business address)*

ADDRESS

CITY   STATE   ZIP

Koh-I-Noor Rapidograph, Inc., 100 North St., Bloomsbury, NJ 08804. In Canada: 1815 Meyerside Dr., Mississauga, Ont. L5T 1G3.

WE BELIEVE WE SELL MORE QUALITY ILLUSTRATION THAN ANYONE ELSE IN THE WORLD. HERE ARE 24 REASONS WHY:

 **RAY AMEIJIDE**

 **MICHAEL DAVID BROWN**

 **LON BUSCH**

 **KEN DALLISON**

 **JACK DAVIS**

 **BOB DESCHAMPS**

 **BILL DEVLIN**

 **RAY DOMINGO**

 **LEE DUGGAN**

 **GINNIE HOFMANN**

 **LIONEL KALISH**

 **LASZLO KUBINYI**

 **LEE LORENZ**

 **ALLAN MARDON**

 **ELWYN MEHLMAN**

 **RANDY GLASS**

 **ALEX MURAWSKI**

 **LOU MYERS**

 **BOB PETERS**

 **JERRY PINKNEY**

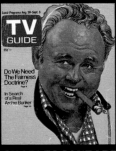 **CHARLES SANTORE**

 **BOB TANENBAUM**

 **MICHAEL WITTE**

 **CAMILLE PRZEWODEK**

GERALD & CULLEN RAPP, INC.
108 East 35 St. (#1), New York 10016
(212) 889-3337 • Fax (212) 889-3341

*FREE FILE BOX

The field's best reference source for contemporary advertising illustration. Write to us on your company letterhead and we will send you our file box. It's packed with miniature color portfolios of our artists' work.

Jim Sharpe

(203) 226·9984

Society of Illustrators
Museum Shop

The Society of Illustrators Museum of American Illustration maintains a shop featuring many quality products. Four-color, large format books document contemporary illustration and the great artists of the past. Catalogues from museum exhibitions highlight specific artists, eras and publications. The Business Library is a must for professionals, young or established. Museum quality prints and posters capture classic images, most available only through The Museum Shop. T-shirts and sweatshirts make practical and fun gifts.

The Museum Shop is an extension of the Society's role as the center for illustration in America today. For further information or quantity discounts, contact the Society at (212) 838-2560.

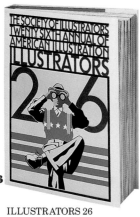

1
ILLUSTRATORS 20
$15.00

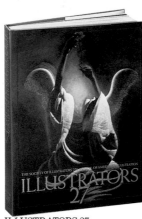

2
ILLUSTRATORS 21
$20.00

3
ILLUSTRATORS 23
$20.00

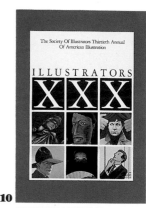

4
ILLUSTRATORS 24
$20.00

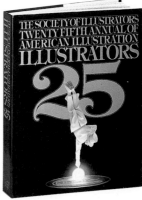

5
ILLUSTRATORS 25
$25.00

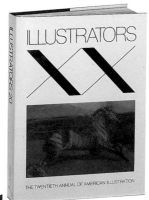

6
ILLUSTRATORS 26
$30.00

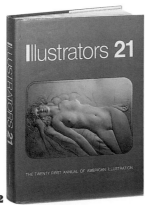

7
ILLUSTRATORS 27
$35.00

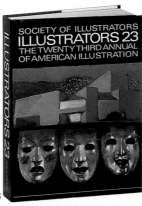

8
ILLUSTRATORS 28
$40.00

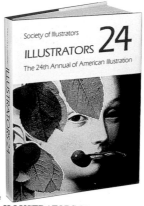

9
ILLUSTRATORS 29
$45.00

10
ILLUSTRATORS 30
$49.95

11
ILLUSTRATORS 31
$49.95

12
200 YEARS OF
AMERICAN ILLUSTRATION
$30.00

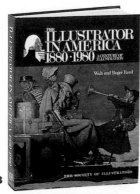

13
THE ILLUSTRATOR IN
AMERICA (1880-1980)
$40.00

14
20 YEARS OF
AWARD WINNERS
$30.00

A limited number of copies of the Illustrators Annuals from 1959 to ILLUSTRATORS 19 are available, as is. Contact the Society for details.

EXHIBITION CATALOGUES These volumes have been created for exhibitions in the Society of Illustrators Museum of American Illustration. They focus on specific artists, eras or subjects.

15

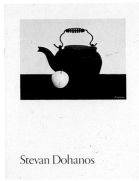

16

17

18

19

COBY WHITMORE – 20pp, color. The good life of the 1950s and 1960s as illustrated in *Ladies' Home Journal, McCall's,* and *Redbook.* $16.00

STEVAN DOHANOS – 36pp, color. The 1986 New Britain Museum of American Art retrospective of the noted *Saturday Evening Post* cover artist. $5.00

ARTHUR I. KELLER – 36pp, B&W. A look at The Belle Epoque and its delineator. $7.50

THE ARTIST EXPLORES OUR WORLD – 32pp, color. The art and biographies of the 60 artists represented in the *National Geographic* centennial exhibition. $5.00

AMERICA'S GREAT WOMEN ILLUSTRATORS (1850-1950) – 24pp, B&W. Decade by decade essays by important historians on the role of women in illustration. $5.00

MUSEUM QUALITY PRINTS Prints of classic works from the Society's Permanent Collection, reproduced on 100% acid free, 100 lb rag paper in an 11 x 14 format. Suitable for framing. $12.00 per print; $38.00 for the set of four

20

J.C. LEYENDECKER
(1874-1951)

21

DEAN CORNWELL
(1892-1960)

22

N.C. WYETH
(1883-1945)

23

MEAD SCHAEFFER
(1898-1980)

THE BUSINESS LIBRARY Each of these volumes is a valuable asset to the professional artist whether established or just starting out. Together they form a solid base for your business.

24

25

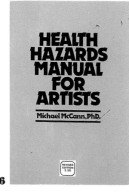

26

THE BUSINESS LIBRARY –
The set of three
volumes – $32.00

GRAPHIC ARTISTS GUILD HANDBOOK, PRICING AND ETHICAL GUIDELINES – Includes an outline of ethical standards and business practices, as well as price ranges for hundreds of uses and sample contracts. $19.95

THE LEGAL GUIDE FOR THE VISUAL ARTIST – Tad Crawford's text explains basic copyrights, moral rights, the sale of rights, taxation, business accounting and the legal support groups available to artists. 1989 Edition. $18.95

HEALTH HAZARDS MANUAL – A comprehensive review of materials and supplies, from fixatives to pigments, airbrushes to solvents. $3.50

ANNUAL EXHIBITION POSTERS The "Call for Entries" poster created each year for the Society's Annual Exhibition. $3.00 each

27
21st Annual –
BOB PEAK
"The Year of
the Horse"

28
25th Annual –
BOB HEINDEL
"Dancer"

29
26th Annual –
MARVIN MATTELSON
"The Unknown
Illustrator"

30
29th Annual –
HODGES SOILEAU
"The Palette"

31
32nd Annual –
ROGER HUYSSEN/
GERARD HUERTA
"Golden Anniversary"

OTHER ARTISTS AVAILABLE: **32.** 24th Annual – BOB CUNNINGHAM "Two Dozen Eggs" **33.** 27th Annual – BARRON STOREY "1984"
34. 28th Annual – WALTER EINSEL/NAIAD EINSEL "Sampler" **35.** 30th Annual – DAVID GROVE "Dreaming" **36.** 31st Annual – BOB McGINNIS "Farmhouse"

SPECIAL EVENT AND EXHIBITION POSTERS

37
"Homage to Howard Pyle –
The Society's 75th
Anniversary" by FRED OTNES

38
"The Illustrator
in America (1880-1980)" by
NORMAN ROCKWELL and
MARK ENGLISH

39
"200 Years of American
Illustration"
by FRED OTNES

40
"Science Fiction"
by JOHN BERKEY

41
"The Art of Medicine"
designed by ART WEITHAS

OTHER ARTISTS AVAILABLE: **42.** "Visions of Flight" by D.K. STONE **43.** "Twenty Years of Award Winners" by MURRAY TINKELMAN
44. "Prizefighters" by BOB PEAK **45.** "Humor 2" by LOU BROOKS **46.** "The Artist Explores our World" by NED SEIDLER. $5.00 each
47. "The Fire of Imagination" by BRAD HOLLAND **48.** "Heartland" by WENDELL MINOR **49.** "The 15th at Oakmont" by DON MOSS
50. "Images" by BRALDT BRALDS. $10.00 each

PRINTS FROM THE HOTEL BARMEN'S ASSOCIATION OF TOKYO CALENDARS These full-color lithographs feature prominent American illustrators interpreting popular cocktails. $5.00 per print

51
GARY KELLEY
"Black Russian"

52
ROBERT GIUSTI
"Americano"

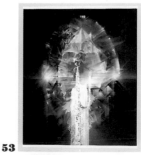

53
BOB PEAK
"Blue Sapphire"

54
MARK ENGLISH
"Angel's Kiss"

55
DOUG JOHNSON
"Irish Coffee"

OTHER ARTISTS AVAILABLE: **56.** BRALDT BRALDS "Cuba Libre" **57.** ALAN E. COBER "Pousse Cafe" **58.** BRAD HOLLAND "Tequila Sunrise" **59.** JIM McMULLAN
"Whiskey Sour" **60.** MURRAY TINKELMAN "Champagne Cocktail"

SI T-SHIRTS Incorporating the Society's logo in three designs (multiple logo, words and lines, large SI). Orange shirts with black lettering. Blue shirts with white lettering. White shirts with two-color lettering. $8.00 each. SIZES: Small, Large, X-Large

61   62   63   64

"Easter" by J.C. LEYENDECKER A special heavyweight cotton, four-color shirt featuring a 1934 *The Saturday Evening Post* cover from the Society's Permanent Collection. $20.00 each. SIZES: Large, X-Large

SI SWEATSHIRTS Blue with white lettering of multiple logo. Grey with large SI. $20.00 each. SIZES: Large, X-Large, XX-Large

65   65

66

SI LAPEL PINS $6.00 – Actual size

ORDER FORM

ENCLOSED IS MY CHECK FOR $_____

Please make check payable to Society of Illustrators.

Name _____

Company (if necessary) _____

Street _____

City _____

State _____ Zip _____

Please charge my credit card:
☐ American Express ☐ MasterCard ☐ Visa

Card number _____

Expiration date _____

Signature _____

Qty	Item #	Price
	1	$15.00
	2	$20.00
	3	$20.00
	4	$20.00
	5	$25.00
	6	$30.00
	7	$35.00
	8	$40.00
	9	$45.00
	10	$49.95
	11	$49.95
	12	$30.00
	13	$40.00
	14	$30.00
	15	$16.00
	16	$ 5.00
	17	$ 7.50
	18	$ 5.00
	19	$ 5.00
	20	$12.00

Qty	Item #	Price
	21	$12.00
	22	$12.00
	23	$12.00
	24	$19.95
	25	$18.95
	26	$ 3.50
	27	$ 5.00
	28	$ 5.00
	29	$ 5.00
	30	$ 5.00
	31	$ 5.00
	32	$ 5.00
	33	$ 5.00
	34	$ 5.00
	35	$ 5.00
	36	$ 5.00
	37	$ 5.00
	38	$ 5.00
	39	$ 5.00
	40	$ 5.00

Qty	Item #	Price
	41	$ 5.00
	42	$ 5.00
	43	$ 5.00
	44	$ 5.00
	45	$ 5.00
	46	$ 5.00
	47	$10.00
	48	$10.00
	49	$10.00
	50	$10.00
	51	$ 5.00
	52	$ 5.00
	53	$ 5.00
	54	$ 5.00
	55	$ 5.00
	56	$ 5.00
	57	$ 5.00
	58	$ 5.00
	59	$ 5.00
	60	$ 5.00

Qty	Item #	Price		
	61	$ 8.00		
Color:		Orange	Blue	White
Size:		Small	Large	X-Large
	62	$ 8.00		
Color:		Orange	Blue	White
Size:		Small	Large	X-Large
	63	$ 8.00		
Color:		Orange	Blue	White
Size:		Small	Large	X-Large
	64	$20.00		
Size:		Large	X-Large	
	65	$20.00		
Color:		Blue	Grey	
Size:		Large	X-Large	XX-Large
				Blue Only
	66	$6.00		
	67	Business Library – **24, 25, & 26** – $32.00		
	68	Set Of Four Prints – **20, 21, 22 & 23** – $38.00		

Total price of item(s) ordered: _____

shipping/handling per order: $2.50

TOTAL DUE: _____

Please mail this form to:
The Society of Illustrators, 128 East 63rd St., New York, NY 10021

Printed in Japan

THE ILLUSTRATOR IN AMERICA 1880·1980

Walt and Roger Reed

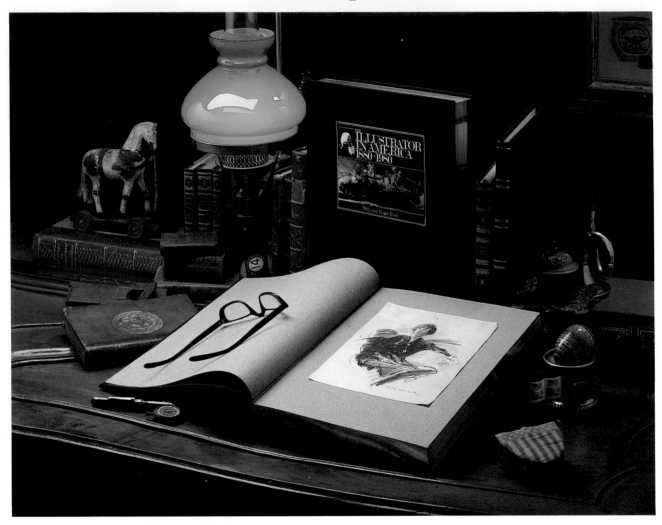

SPECIAL LIMITED EDITIONS

**The Society of Illustrators is proud to offer
a limited edition of signed and numbered volumes of
The Illustrator in America 1880-1980 by Walt and Roger Reed.**

Each contains an original work by one of three famous illustrators:
F.R. Gruger   John Held, Jr.   Harry Beckhoff

This special limited edition gives you an original work of art for your collection plus an exquisite volume for your library. Each Gruger, Held and Beckhoff is hand-tipped in on special stock in gilt-edged, handsomely boxed editions of *The Illustrator in America 1880-1980*. All are signed and numbered. Autographed by the authors, every volume also has the purchaser's name embossed in gold on the cover.

The author, Walt Reed, is the preeminent illustration historian who has written volumes on such notables as Harold Von Schmidt, John Clymer and Joseph Clement Coll. With his son Roger, he owns Illustration House, Inc., a gallery devoted entirely to the work of illustrators. Together the Reeds have recorded the lives and

exhibited the works of every important artist from 1880-1980. From early masters like Howard Pyle, Charles Dana Gibson and N.C. Wyeth, to the Golden Days of Frederic Remington, Maxfield Parrish, Norman Rockwell, Stevan Dohanos and, more contemporarily, Bernard Fuchs, Milton Glaser and Brad Holland.

Each decade in the book is introduced by a famous illustrator with comprehensive knowledge of the period. This exciting volume provides historical facts, personality insights and examples by the great illustrators. Our special limited edition provides an opportunity to possess an original illustration by three of the most important artists of the last century.

**The deluxe, 9 x 12 editions, containing over 700 illustrations on 352 pages,
half in full color, are a complete pictorial and biographical record
of the greatest illustrators in America from 1880 to 1980.**

F.R. Gruger: approximately 4" x 7"

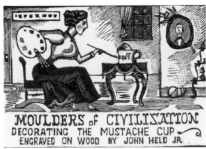

John Held Jr.: actual size 4 3/4" x 3 1/4"

Harry Beckhoff: approximately 3" x 2"

250 ORIGINAL F.R. GRUGER DRAW-INGS, estate-signed and numbered, tipped into special, limited editions of THE ILLUSTRATOR IN AMERICA 1880-1980, autographed by Walt and Roger Reed. An illustrator's illustrator, Gruger is on a par with Pyle, Wyeth and Gibson. In the Society of Illustrators Hall of Fame, he is a recognized master.

50 JOHN HELD, JR. WOODBLOCK PRINTS. From a one-of-a-kind edition of 100, these prints are signed by Mrs. John Held, Jr. and tipped into autographed copies of THE ILLUSTRA-TOR IN AMERICA 1880-1980. Harold Ross, famed *New Yorker* editor, commissioned Held to do satirical studies of the Victorian era. This is one of the finest examples.

200 ORIGINAL HARRY BECKHOFF DRAWINGS, signed by the artist and numbered, tipped into special, limited editions of THE ILLUSTRATOR IN AMERICA 1880-1980 and auto-graphed by Walt and Roger Reed. These jewel-like thumbnail sketches contain all the necessary information for the final artwork. Beckhoff is best known for his Damon Runyan characters for *Collier's*.

*ALL SPECIAL VOLUMES ARE ELEGANTLY BOXED, AUTOGRAPHED BY
THE AUTHORS AND EMBOSSED WITH THE NAME OF THE PURCHASER.*

- -

Order Your Copy of THE ILLUSTRATOR IN AMERICA 1880-1980...Today

___volume(s) of THE ILLUSTRATOR IN AMERICA 1880-1980 by Walt and Roger Reed containing one of 250 original drawings by F.R. GRUGER, hand-tipped on special stock, estate-signed, autographed by the authors, with purchaser's name embossed in gold and handsomely boxed.

$150.00

___volume(s) of THE ILLUSTRATOR IN AMERICA 1880-1980 by Walt and Roger Reed containing one of 200 original drawings by HARRY BECKHOFF, hand-tipped on special stock, signed by the artist, autographed by the authors, with purchaser's name embossed in gold and handsomely boxed.

$75.00

___volume(s) of THE ILLUSTRATOR IN AMERICA 1880-1980 by Walt and Roger Reed containing one of 100 original woodcuts by JOHN HELD, JR., hand-tipped on special stock, signed by Mrs. John Held, Jr., auto-graphed by the authors, with purchaser's name embossed in gold and handsomely boxed.

$50.00

___Plus $2.50 per copy for postage and handling. Please make checks payable to:

Madison Square Press, Inc.
10 East 23rd Street
New York City, NY 10010

Charge my credit card plus $2.50 per copy for postage and handling.

Check one:

☐ **American Express**

☐ **Visa**

☐ **Master Charge**

Number_____

_____

Exp. date_____

Name _____

Address _____

City _____

State _____ **Zip** _____

Signature _____

New York State residents add 8.25% sales tax.